COOL PEDAL STEEL LICKS FOR GUITAR

BY TOBY WINE

PLAYBACK+
Speed · Pitch · Balance · Loop

To access audio visit:
www.halleonard.com/mylibrary

2048-4292-2384-3621

Recording Credits: Toby Wine, Guitar

ISBN: 978-1-57560-533-3

Visit Hal Leonard Online at
www.halleonard.com

Table of Contents

Introduction

About This Book

The pedal steel guitar has been called "the heart of country music," and it's a versatile and complex instrument equally capable of lyrical melodies, atmospheric clouds of sound, and virtuoso solo flights. Countless country and Western recordings have been enriched and filled with gorgeous detail by the often-unassuming men and women toiling away with steel bar in hand, knees and feet working the pedals and levers, while seated behind one of these odd, intimidating machines. In recent days the pedal steel and its players have begun to command a bigger portion of the spotlight and the ears of a broader and expanding audience. The popularity of alternative country is at an all time high, and rock, folk, gospel, and jazz artists have begun to include the instrument on recordings and in touring bands, introducing it to new listeners and taking it to places it has rarely gone before. The aim of this humble book is to introduce electric guitarists to the world of sounds and effects possible with pedal steel and put a little bit of that magic under their fingers, using standard tunings and setups, eschewing the use of glass or metal slides, b-benders, capos, and other devices. All that you'll need is your guitar, good ears, patience, and the desire to expand your arsenal to include these fascinating and beautiful sounds.

The pedal steel guitar evolved slowly, and has roots that can be traced back to the acoustic Hawaiian slack key guitar playing of the late 19th and early 20th centuries, through to the advent of the lap steel guitar and the addition of those pedals and knee levers that bring such mystery and adaptability to the instrument we hear today. The modern pedal steel features one or (often) two guitar-style necks laid horizontally across a tabletop surface supported by four legs. Beneath the tabletop, rods extend down to foot pedals and knee levers that are used to raise or lower individual strings or groups of strings much like a harp. The most common contemporary setup, thanks in large part to virtuoso trailblazer Buddy Emmons, features two ten-string necks tuned to E9 and C6 chords. The player holds a smoothly-rounded, heavyweight steel bar in the left hand, sliding from fret to fret to sound single lines, double stops, and chords, while the back of the hand trails behind, muting unplayed strings and stopping excessive jangle and sympathetic vibrations—much like a slide guitarist would. The right hand, equipped with steel fingerpicks, sounds the notes and aids in the muting of unused strings simultaneously. All the while, pitches are raised and lowered with the pedals and levers below, allowing for a fully chromatic, fully expressive music to emerge.

Emulating the sound of the pedal steel is no easy task. Essentially, the guitarist must change his or her approach from that of a fretted instrument with discrete pitches to one where notes and chords slide smoothly from one to another, and tones ring out on some strings while they move on others. Techniques include extensive sliding, hammer-ons, pull-offs, bending, and especially prebends, where a string is bent up silently to a specific pitch and then struck and held or released down in a legato, vocal fashion (in simulation of a steeler's pitch-dropping pedals). The examples that follow—a collection of licks, tricks, exercises, chord workouts, and complete solo statements—represent the mere tip of the iceberg of what is possible with this fascinating approach. With a little imagination, this book can serve as a stepping-stone to the creation of your own unique and beautiful music, and hopefully open doors to new sounds and skills on your own guitar.

A Word of Caution

Much of the material in this book is both musically and physically demanding, and it is imperative that it is approached slowly and with care. The musical challenges mostly involve the development of a strong sense of intonation; those prebends must be in tune, or you'll sound more like your average overzealous string-bending guitar slinger than a smooth and lyrical steeler. The physical challenges, on the other hand, involve stretches, hammers, pulls, and repeated bends that are often held while other fingers work on other strings, which can result in repetitive stress trauma to the fretting hand. If you experience pain or stiffness, put the guitar down and rest for a while. If you really injure yourself, you may have to lay off for an extended period, and it's just not worth it. The last thing you want is to give yourself a nasty case of tendonitis, carpal tunnel syndrome, or any other incapacitating malady. Stretch your hands and fingers gently before picking up the guitar, and then perform a slow and measured warm-up routine before diving in, taking care that your hands are strong, relaxed, and ready to work.

Some Thoughts on Equipment

The examples that follow are designed to be played on any standard-tuned six-string electric guitar, but there are some guidelines that can help you to get quicker, better results. For one, unless you are a physical monster, a guitar with light gauge strings and low action—an easy playing setup—is preferable, as it allows for easier string bending and vibrato and will minimize the wear and tear on the muscles and tendons in your hands. A fixed bridge/tailpiece (non-tremolo) will allow for more pitch stability as well; a whammy bar–equipped guitar, especially a floating unit such as a Floyd Rose, will drift as strings are bent while others remain stationary. Any good, clear-toned amp will do the trick, although if you're planning to crank it up, be sure it won't distort. Steelers often use a fairly *wet* sound (i.e., lots of reverb) and frequently employ a digital delay device, especially on the more atmospheric ballad parts. The use of a volume pedal to add sustain to decaying pitches and a general ethereal breathiness is also quite common. Effects and setups aside, the most important aspect of emulation is listening. Pedal steel has a very distinctive sound, and only through careful and attentive listening to a variety of recordings is a faithful recreation of that sound possible. There are phrases, dynamics, attack, and especially vibrato that are unique to and characteristic of the instrument, and you'll need to get all of this into your ears before you can truly hope to achieve success.

Track 1

Note: Track 1 contains tuning pitches.

About the Author

Toby Wine lives in New York City and is a freelance guitarist, composer, and author. A graduate of the Manhattan School of Music, Toby's compositions and arrangements can be heard on recordings by Phillip Harper (Muse), Ari Ambrose (Steeplechase), and Ian Hendrickson Smith (Kpasta and Fresh Sound). He splits his time between live performances, studio recordings, arranging, teaching, and writing. His Cherry Lane publications include *The Art of Texas Blues, 1001 Blues Licks, Metallica Under the Microscope,* and many others. His studies have included work with Walter Davis Jr., Manny Albam, Bob Mover, Bern Nix, Ken Wessel, and Edward Green. He currently appears around town with the R&B/salsa band Melee and as a sideman with a variety of jazz and pop ensembles.

Acknowledgments

I'd like to express my appreciation to Susan Poliniak, Mark Phillips, and the rest of the team at Cherry Lane, Mom, Dad, Bibi, Bob, Jack, Lissette, Enid, the online pedal steel community (a tremendous resource), all of my patient friends and colleagues, and especially my dear friend, guitarist, pedal steel player, and captain of industry Sam Minnitti, without whose generous and informed consultancy this project would not have been possible.

Essential Techniques and Exercises

This quest for pedal steel simulation begins with a variety of exercises designed to get your hands and ears in shape and ready to go. Many of the exercises that follow either build finger strength through a variety of bending techniques, or work to improve bending intonation by matching pitches with open strings or other stationary (i.e., unbent) notes. Steelers often play two or more notes and then hit a pedal or lever, dropping the pitch of one of the strings. In order for you to achieve this effect on electric guitar, you'll have to do an awful lot of *prebending*, where a given string is bent up to a specified pitch before it is struck. Intonation is crucial here, as is a great deal of muscle memory—you'll need to know precisely how far to bend a string without hearing it first!

Notice, by the way, that the accompanying audio tracks are split-channel. You can pan your playback device to one side to hear a lick demonstrated, or to the other side to play the lick along with a rhythm guitar.

Unison Bending Exercise

This exercise matches whole step bends with fretted notes on an adjacent upper string. Execute all of the bends with your ring finger and allow the strings to ring for their full durations. Loop the example repeatedly and work slowly. Speed is meaningless if the notes aren't clean and in tune. This one will reveal how accurate your string bending really is!

Track 2

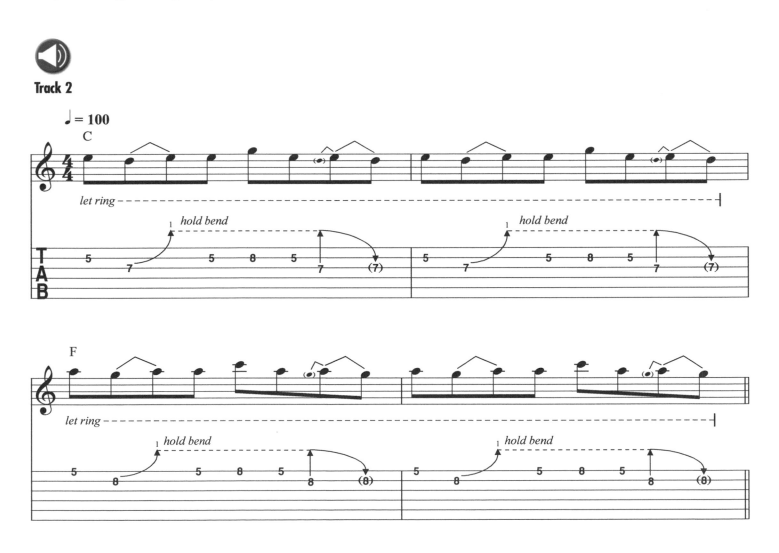

Pitch-Matching Exercise with Vibrato

This exercise pairs the droning open low E string with ascending E major scale pitches on the B string. You'll want to use your fingers or a combination of pick and fingers to play notes on two strings that are far apart. On the final, tied note in each measure, wait briefly before adding light vibrato (a practice common to pedal-steelers), mimicking the action of a steel guitarist. The open string serves as a point of reference for pitch-bending accuracy.

Track 3

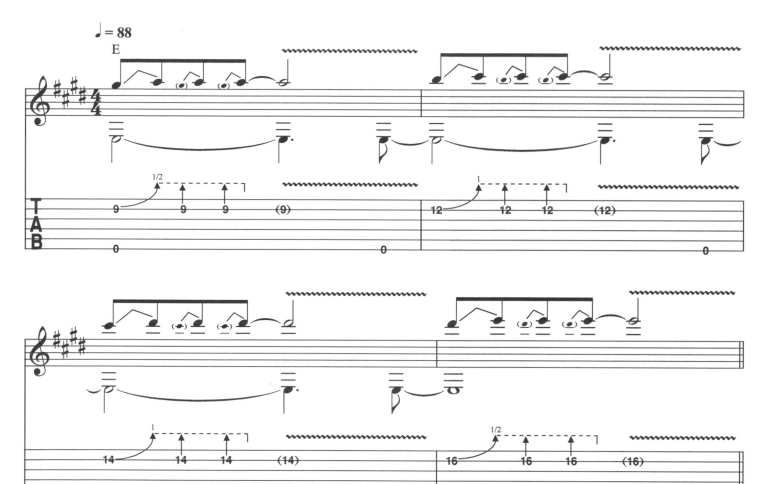

Pitch-Matching Exercise with Stationary Upper Note

This exercise is extremely similar to the preceding one, except this time the stationary note is *above* the bends. As with the previous example, wait briefly before applying vibrato. Play the first bend with your ring finger while your index finger plays the B on the high E string; the three bends that follow should be executed by your middle finger, with the ring finger handling the higher pitches.

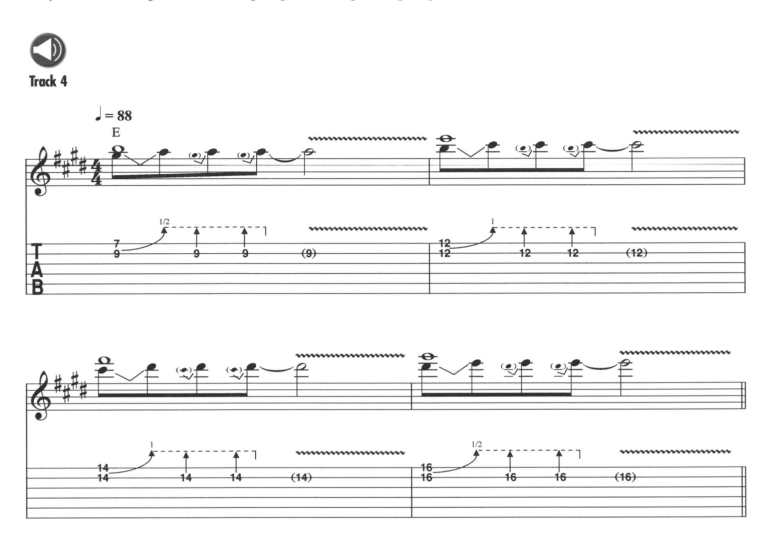

Track 4

Downward Bending Exercise in D Major

This exercise combines bends that are pulled toward the floor with pitch-matching between the open D string and fretted notes on the G string. Besides helping you with your sense of intonation, this will get you used to the differing amounts of strength needed to execute bends as you climb and descend a single string.

Track 5

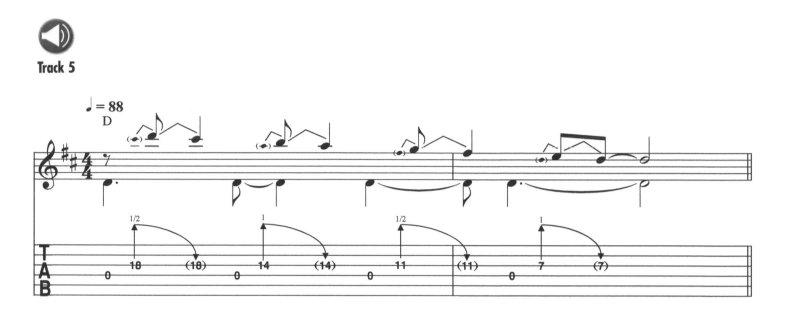

Downward Bending Exercise in A Major

This exercise is highly similar to the previous one, except that it involves the open A string and descending prebend-and-release figures on the D string. Notice the difference in strength needed to accurately bend the D and G strings!

Track 6

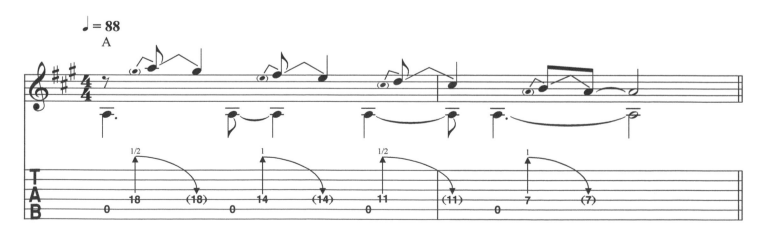

Downward Bending Exercise in C Major

This exercise descends the A and G strings in 6ths—use your fingers or a combination of fingers and pick. The pitches on the A string follow the C major scale as it descends, while your index finger bends the G string up and down. All of the bends in this exercise should be pulled toward your feet.

Track 7

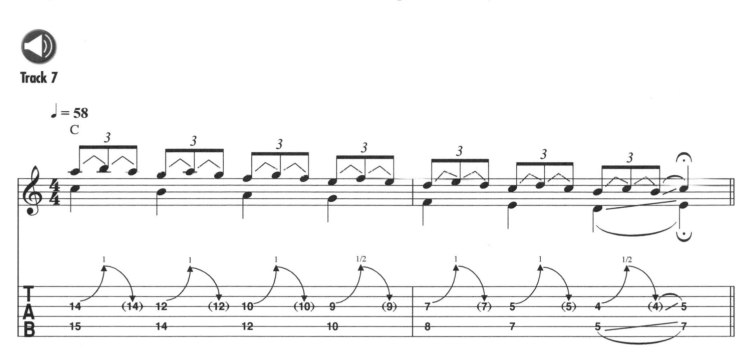

Prebent Descending C Major Scale

This exercise descends the C major scale (beginning with its 3rd, E) along the B string. There are four prebends along the way; play all but the last with your ring finger. After releasing from F to E in measure 3, prebend the G string (5th fret) up to D, and then release to the tonic, C, while the E continues to ring on the B string.

Track 8

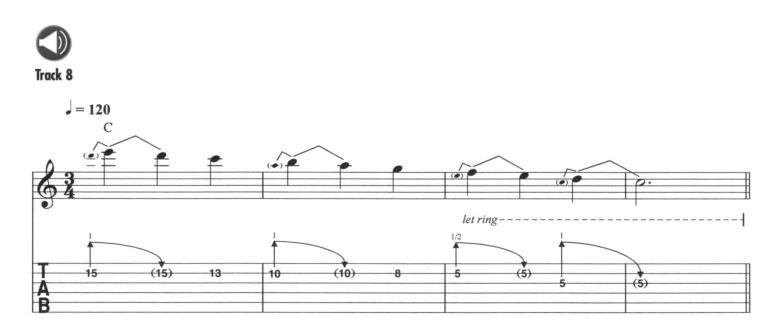

Ascending Scale Exercise in C Major

This exercise both ascends and descends a one-octave C major scale. Begin by sliding your ring finger along the G string from the 5th to the 7th fret before executing a whole step bend. Shift to the B string (6th fret) with your index finger; here, bend the G up to A with your ring finger and push the 7th up to the octave (E string, 7th fret) with your middle finger. Play all of the prebends on the descent with your ring finger.

Track 9

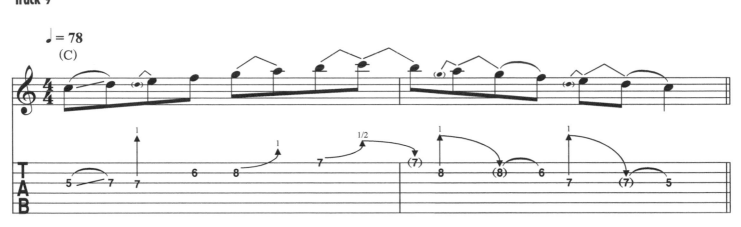

Prebending Pattern in A Major

Here's another prebend exercise that pairs an open string (A) with fretted notes on a higher string (G), thus allowing you to check the pitch accuracy of your bends along the way. Each prebend should be executed by your ring finger, and then released and pulled off to your index finger (for whole step pull-offs) or middle finger (for half steps). The final prebend to the A two octaves above the open A string should be played with the middle finger. Note that you might want to "tug" the strings a bit with your left-hand fingers as you pull-off—you'll hear this sort of articulation often in this book (and in the style).

Track 10

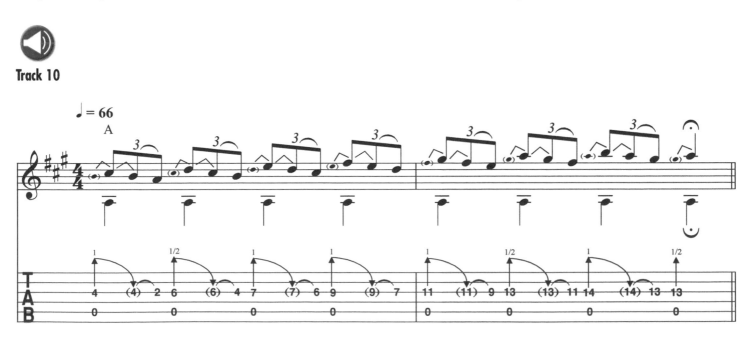

Ringing Prebend

In a preview of licks to come, this simple phrase begins with your pinky at the 8th fret of the high E string while your ring finger executes a prebend-and-release along the B string. Pull off to your index finger and slide down a fret to E without picking. The high C should ring throughout the phrase.

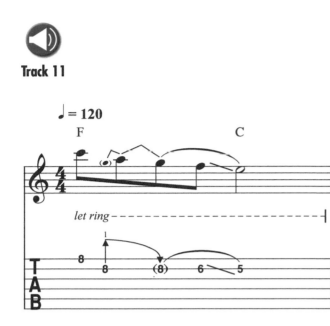

Track 11

Prebending Scale Pattern in A Major

Here's a simple descending phrase in A major that's designed to get those ubiquitous prebends in tune and under your fingers. Play all but the last bend with your ring finger; the G-string bend should be executed by your middle finger. You can hit the open A string before beginning the phrase to check your intonation.

Track 12

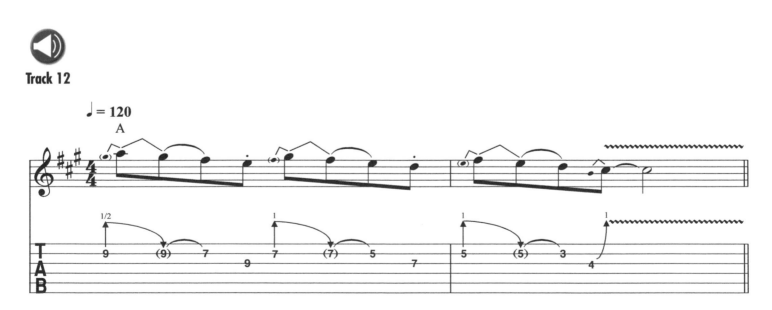

Ring-Finger Exercise

This exercise begins with a whole step ring-finger bend on the G string that is held and followed by pitches on the B and high E strings before being released. As you follow the pattern up the fingerboard, be sure to arch your fingers enough to allow the notes in each measure to ring out for their full durations while the bend is held.

Track 13

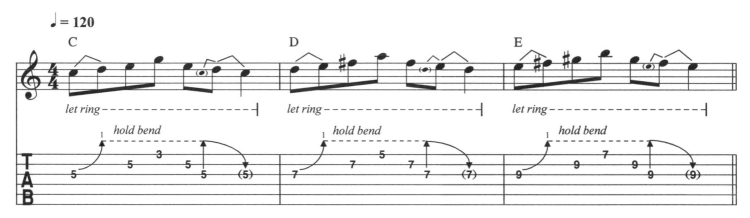

Ringing Prebend Pattern in D Major

This set of ascending four-note phrases outlines the ii, iii, IV, and V chords in the key of D major. Loop the example around on itself, let each string ring throughout, and play the first-measure prebends with your ring finger and the second-measure prebends with your middle finger. Be careful not to push the second prebend too far—it's only a half step!

Track 14

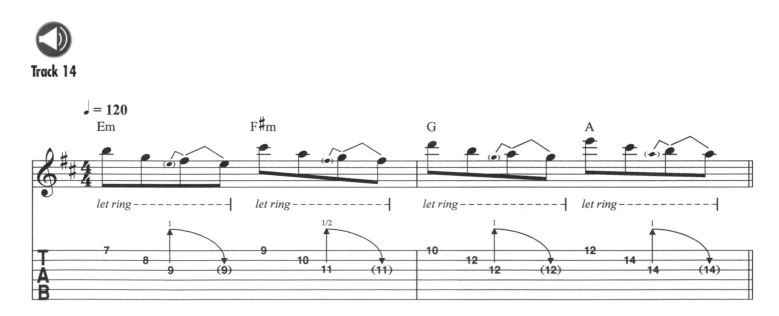

Chromatic 6ths

These chromatically ascending 6ths, spaced a string apart, are common in country and country/rock solos—but they're not easy! The difficulty lies in getting your bends in tune in a chromatic context, where they're much more difficult to hear. Work slowly and play the notes on the high E string with your pinky while your middle finger executes the G-string bends.

Track 15

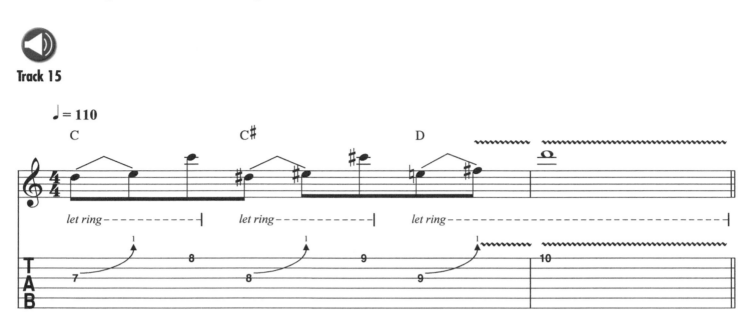

Pinky Bend

Pick (or grab) the top three strings on this one only once. Begin with your middle and ring fingers on the B and high E strings, respectively, while your pinky prebends and releases the G string and then pulls off to your index finger. Finish by pushing the G string up a whole step with your index finger without picking again.

Track 16

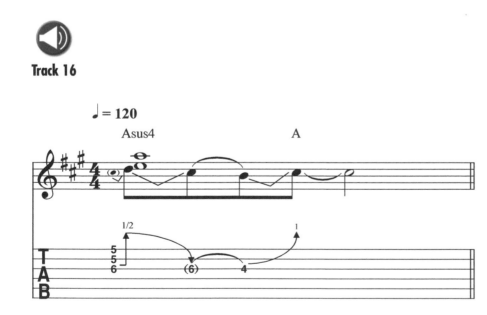

Middle-Finger Strength Builder

This two-measure phrase over A7 is more like a cool lick than an exercise, but it really helps to build bending strength in the middle finger. Use your pinky for the 3rd of the chord (on the high E string), with your middle finger executing the repeated B-string bends and your ring finger grabbing the lone note on the G string.

Track 17

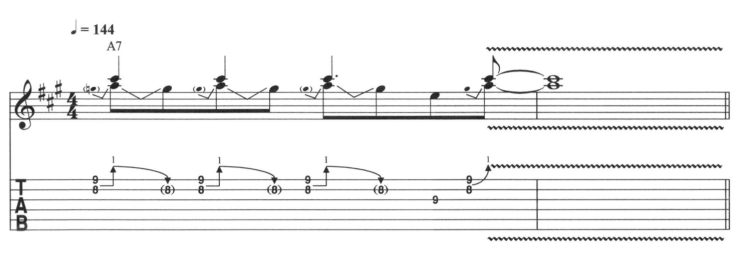

Harmony Bend Exercise

This exercise gets you bending two strings at once, and should be repeated, like any other exercise, until you can play it cleanly, smoothly, and in tune. Use your middle and ring fingers on the B and G strings, respectively, and slide the grip up two frets to hear your target tones before beginning. The key is in maintaining a fair amount of rigidity in the grip so that each string is bent upwards with equal strength. The phrase finishes with a middle-finger suspension-release prebend, while your index finger barres the top two strings.

Track 18

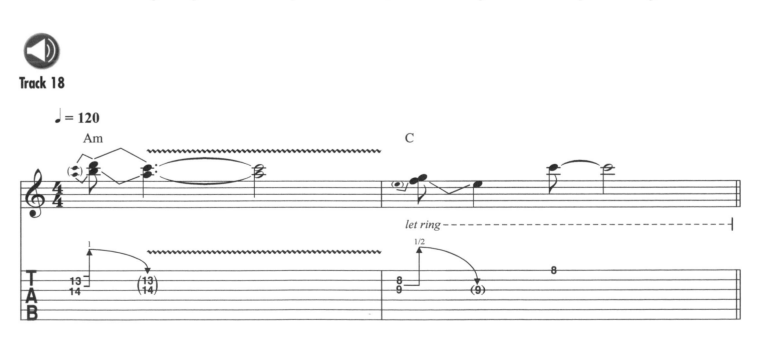

Sliding Parallel Chords

These sliding, rootless dominant chords should be picked (or grabbed) just once, letting the slides do the rest of the work. Press down firmly with your fretting fingers and keep the pressure consistent to sound each chord. Try tweaking the last chord with a little swell of a volume knob or pedal. Steelers slide like this constantly, often using diminished or augmented forms. Don't worry—we'll get back to these later. In the meantime, make up some sliding combinations of your own.

Track 19

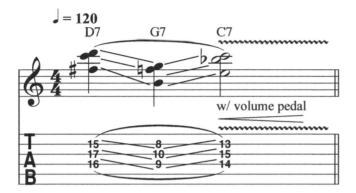

Descending Resolutions

These suspension-and-release figures, descending in whole steps from E, may not be typical pedal steel material but they come in handy and give you another chance to work on your middle-finger bending technique. Use that digit for all of the half step bends while your pinky and index fingers grab the notes on the B and high E strings, respectively. The differences in strength required to execute whole and half step bends on each string vary in subtle but important degrees, and it's important to know how much strength is required with your particular technique and instrument.

Track 20

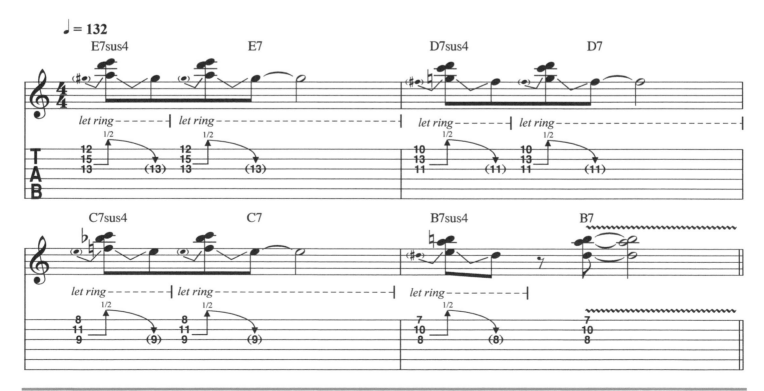

Chord Cycle Exercise

This jazzy chord cycle provides a good example of the type of beautiful inner-voice resolution possible with prebends, and loosely simulates the pedal steel *pads* (long, sustained chords) found in some of the more harmonically sophisticated ballads. The phrase alternates between middle-finger and index-finger prebend-and-releases. In the final measure, pull off to the 12th fret on the B string via your pinky to your ring finger.

Track 21

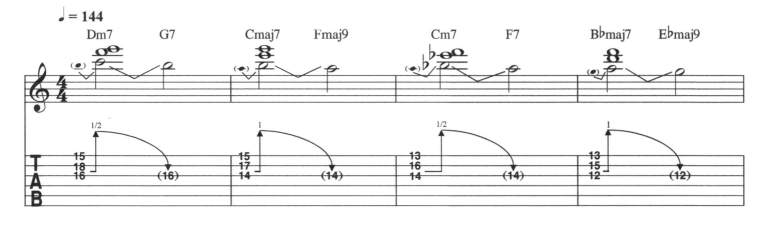

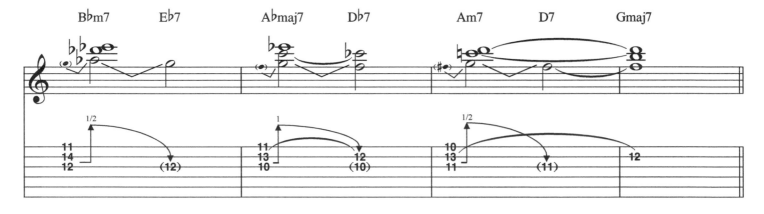

Volume Swell Exercise #1

The volume pedal is almost like an instrument unto itself, and the depth of its expressiveness will be matched by your diligence in practicing with it. It should be noted that most steelers use custom or specially designed pedals intended for use with their particular instrument; pedals such as these are much more sensitive and require significantly less rocking to create swells and fades. Essentially, a pedal is never "off" or "on"—it just moves subtly between "somewhat louder" and "somewhat softer." It is used most prominently in ballad playing, creating ghostly effects, and drawing out the sustain of decaying chords. Luckily for us guitar players, many of our volume pedals now feature adjustable sensitivity to help us get closer to the pedal steel sound. In this (very slow!) exercise, pay close attention to the crescendo and decrescendo markings; they will let you know when to give the pedal some juice and when to back off. Obviously, this exercise and the one that follows are just the tip of the iceberg of potential exercises and effects—let your creativity take you on a journey that ebbs and flows like the ocean!

Track 22

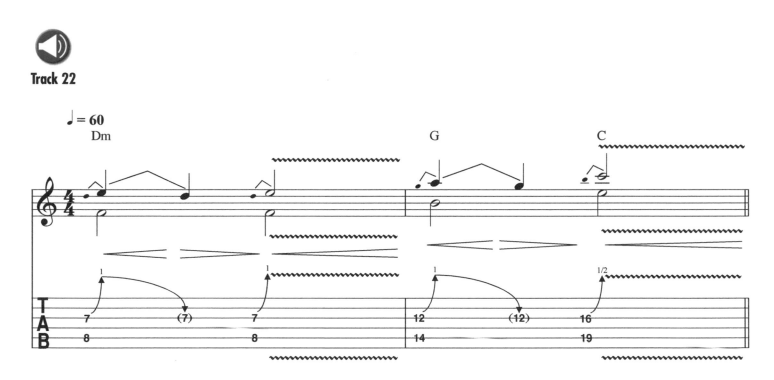

Volume Swell Exercise #2

Here's another simple volume-pedal phrase using three-note chords and *oblique bends* (one string is bent while others that are played at the same time remain "stationary"). All of the bending here should be done with your middle finger backed up by your index finger. Follow the crescendo and decrescendo markings to guide you in the use of the pedal—but remember that exercises like this one (and every other example in this book, for that matter) can take you only so far. You must spend time listening to live performances and recordings of pedal steel players to get the sound and feel of this unique instrument.

Track 23

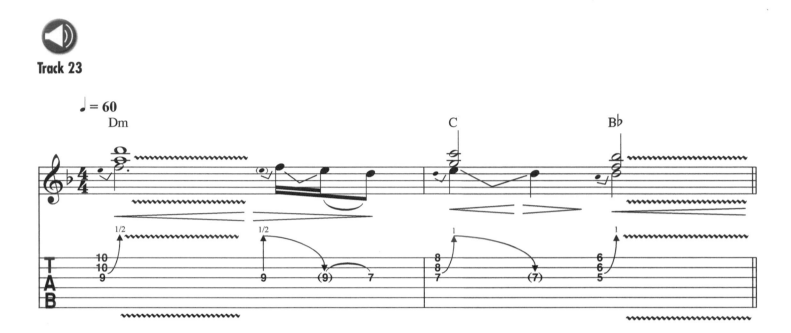

Short Licks and Phrases

Let's start making some music with the techniques you've learned so far. These quick licks and fragments put together much of what's been examined already and aim to get you thinking of these techniques as tools for making beautiful, pedal steel–inspired music. Be sure to take any example you particularly enjoy and learn to play it in all keys, registers, and tempos. It needs to be under your fingers and in your ears if you want to access it later in a musical, uncontrived fashion.

Easy Major Lick

Here's a super-common major lick that's right in the country style. After the three-note pick-up, use your middle finger to execute the prebend, release, pull-off, and re-bend (!) on the G string while your ring finger and pinky remain in place on the B and high E strings, respectively.

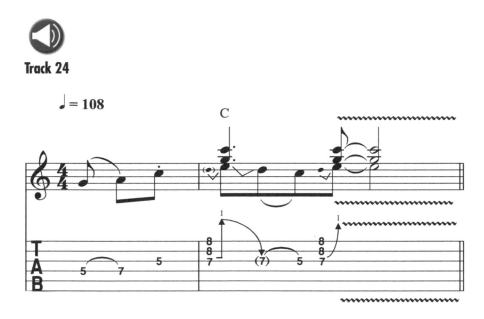

Track 24

A Major/E Major Phrase

This sunny little lick could actually be in A major (I–V progression) or E major (IV–I). Begin with a G-string hammer-on, follow with an index-finger slide from the 9th to the 10th fret of the B string, and then use your ring finger to execute the whole step bend-and-hold at the 12th fret. Play the final double stop with your ring finger on the B string while your middle finger bends the G string.

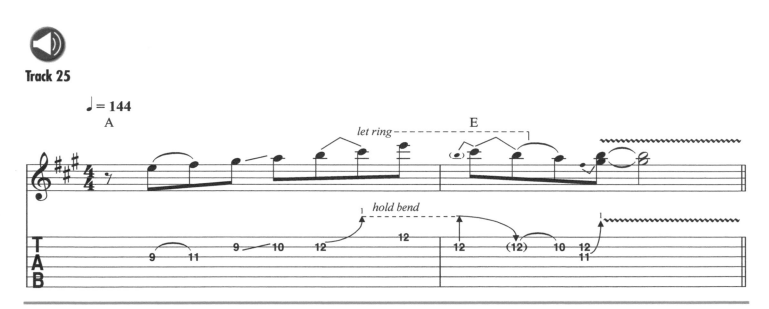

Track 25

Oblique Bend with Sliding Double Stop

This attractive little lick requires you to hold a G-string bend with your ring finger while you play notes on the B and high E strings with your pinky and index fingers. Make sure that bend is held fast—if you let it sag at all, nobody will miss your bad intonation, and it certainly won't sound like pedal steel! Pedals and levers (to a great extent) hold their notes in place on that instrument, but you must work that much harder on yours.

Track 26

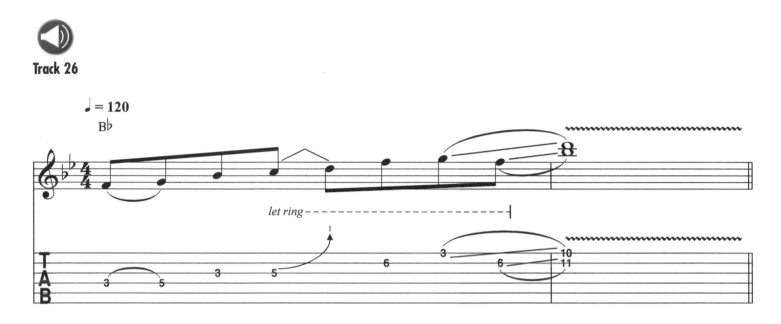

Pivoting Lick

Here's another one that requires you to hold bent notes—this time, on the B string with the middle finger—while playing other pitches on a higher string. Again, hold that B-string bend rigid while executing the pull-offs above it to achieve a real pedal steel effect.

Track 27

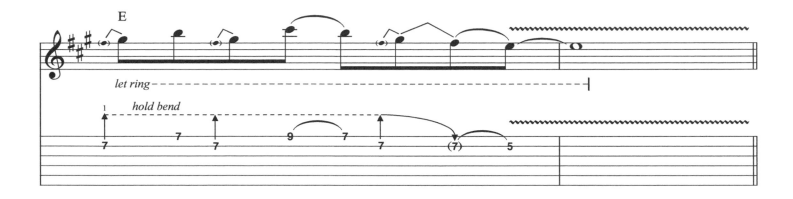

Harmony Bend and Double Stops

This pretty phrase uses the two-string bending technique touched upon in the previous chapter, as well as some tasty E major double stops and slides. Before beginning, move your first grip up two frets to hear your target tones, and then execute the bends smoothly but very firmly and evenly, ensuring that each string is raised a precise whole step. Remember that the more your sense of intonation falters, the more you'll sound like a sloppy amateur instead of an accomplished pedal-steeler! Wrap the lick up by using your index finger to slide the first two eighth notes down in measure 2, and then add your ring finger for the A-string bend-and-release.

Track 28

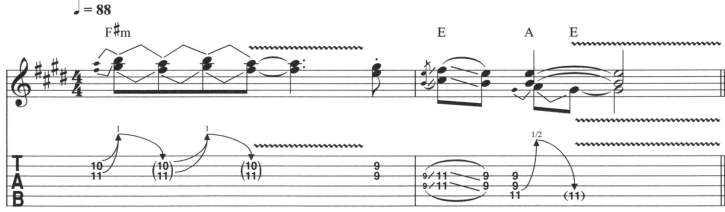

Quick ii–V–I Lick

Here's a simple phrase for a ii–V–I or another turnaround in B♭ major (or any key you transpose it to). Use your ring finger for the first prebend; release and pull off to your index finger. While E♭ sustains on the B string, use your middle finger to create the G-string prebend, providing a brief but tasty half step rub between D and E♭.

Track 29

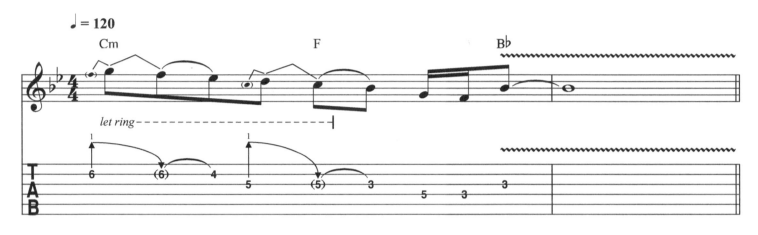

Slow ii–V Lick

This one fits nicely over a ballad-tempo ii–V in G major. As with the previous example, bend and pull off from your ring to index finger, and then play the B-string prebend while the higher string continues to ring.

Track 30

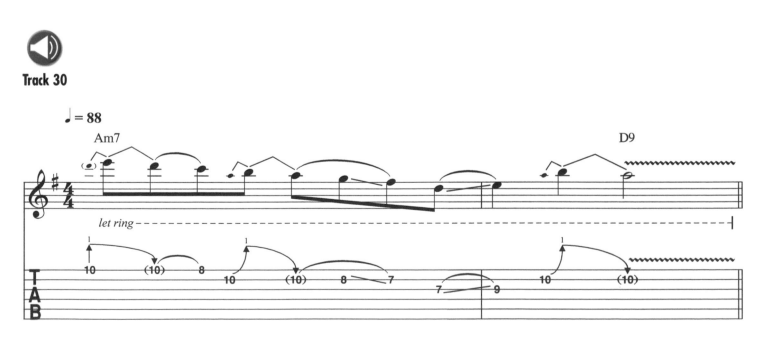

ii–V–I–IV Lick with Double Stops

This simple phrase, based on a common chord progression, uses double stops and simple eighth note lines to outline the harmony. Play the first bend with your ring finger, the second with your middle finger (with your pinky on the high E string), and the third with your ring finger; play the G-string bend in measure 3 with your middle finger. Be sure to apply a little tasty vibrato to simulate the steel guitarist's "shake" of the bar.

Track 31

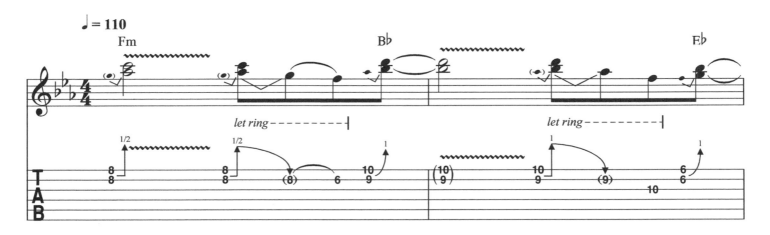

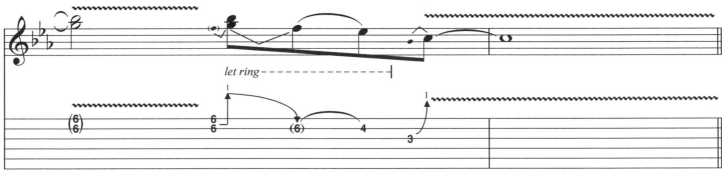

V–IV–I Lick

Work this simple eighth note lick up to a fairly brisk tempo and use it over a V–IV–I turnaround in G major, or any other place you can hear it fitting in. Be sure to observe the "let ring" markings throughout and you'll generate a little harmony as you go—the half step rub between C and B in the last group of eighth notes is particularly tasty.

Track 32

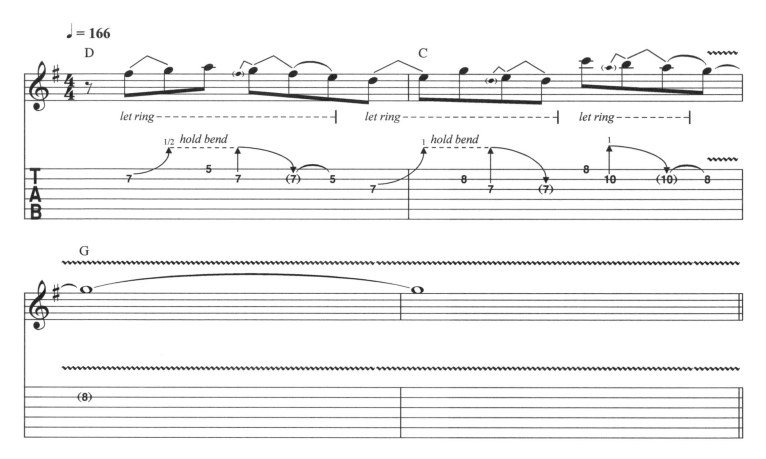

Bluesy Dominant Lick

The half step bend that begins this simple lick gives you a #9 sound over a dominant chord, but it's combined with notes taken from the A major pentatonic scale (A–B–C#–E–F#) to create a sort of hybrid sound that's very common to country and country/rock soloing. Try to allow the high E to ring for the duration of the lick so it can still be heard in harmony with the G–A prebend that ends the phrase.

Track 33

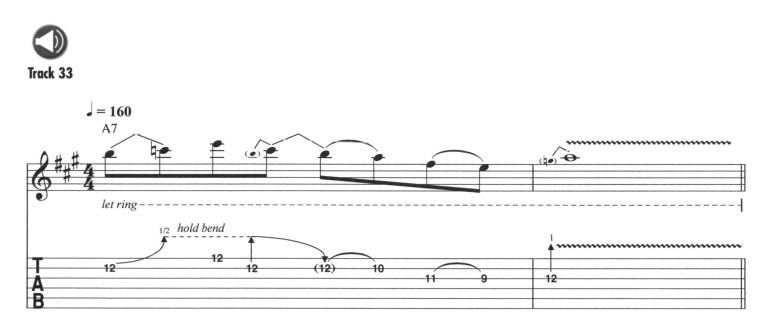

Ascending Prebend Lick

More B- and E-string hijinks here. A lick like this, with its slightly chicken-picked major and minor 2nd intervals, is just a glimpse of what's possible with fast, simulated steel sounds along two strings. Use your index finger to play all of the notes on the high E string and your ring finger for each prebend.

Track 34

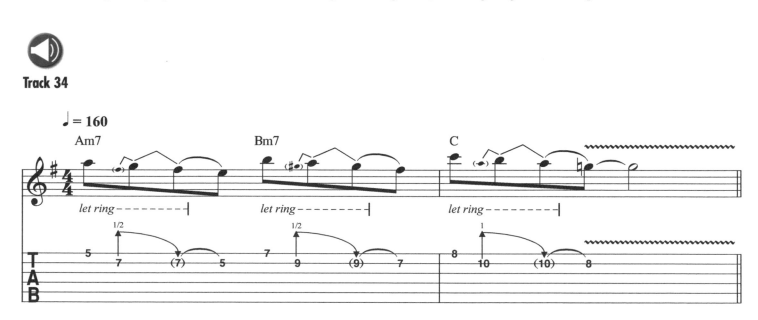

G Minor Pattern

Here's a simple descending phrase in G minor with more ring-finger bending. To play the final four-note grouping of eighth notes, begin with your index finger at the 5th fret of the high E string, bend the B string (6th fret) up a half step with your middle finger, and then move both up to the minor 3rd double stop that completes the phrase.

Track 35

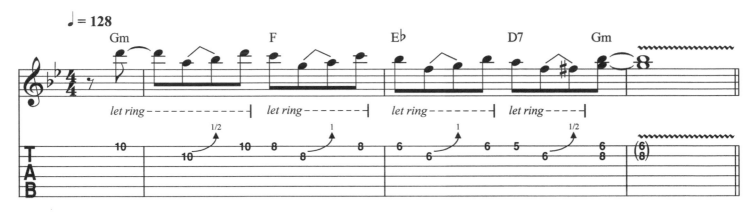

G Minor Lick in 6ths

Here's an example of how sliding 6ths can be used in a minor context, rather than in major, in which it is more commonly encountered. Take the first prebend with your middle finger, slide down the high E string from C to B♭ with your index finger, prebend with your middle finger again, and then shift positions so that the A that begins the second measure is played by your ring finger. The final bend can be played with either the index or middle finger.

Track 36

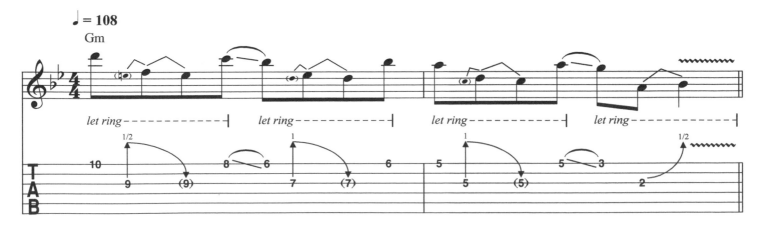

C Minor Lick

Use your ring finger for all of the bending in this pretty C minor phrase except for the final G-string bend. The B and high E strings should still be ringing when you use your middle finger to push F up to G.

Track 37

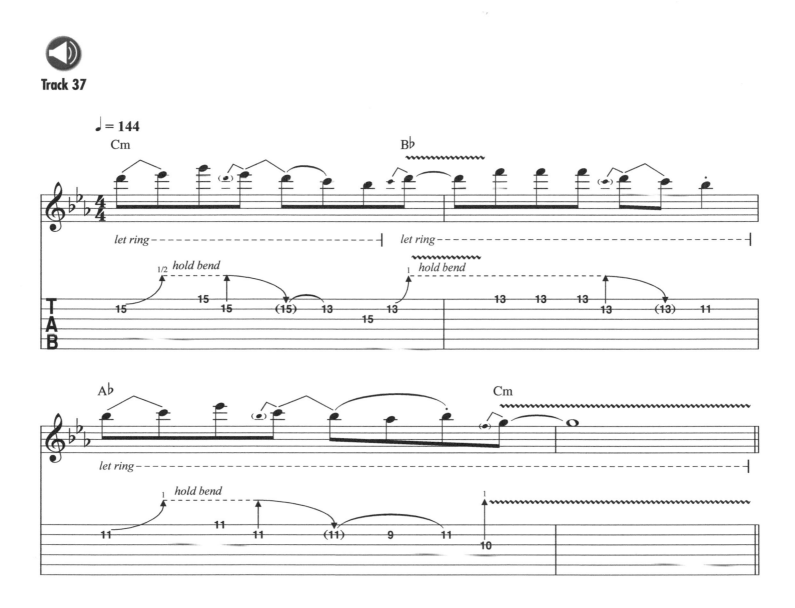

E Major Lick with Open-String Unison Bend

This lick ends with a unison between the bent B string and the open high E string—a very steely effect indeed. Begin the example with a ring-finger bend, and then shift so the final eighth note in the first measure is played by your pinky. Follow with a ring-finger prebend-and-release, shift again to grab the A with your pinky, and wrap things up by bending the B string up a half step with your middle finger to create the E unison effect.

Track 38

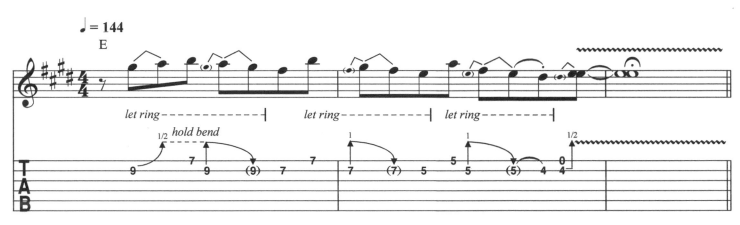

B Major Lick with Open-String Unison Bend

Here's another short lick that finishes with a unison flourish. Begin with a ring-finger bend that's held while your pinky and index fingers grab the notes on the high E string, and then shift positions at the start of the second measure to grab the 12th-fret B with your pinky.

Track 39

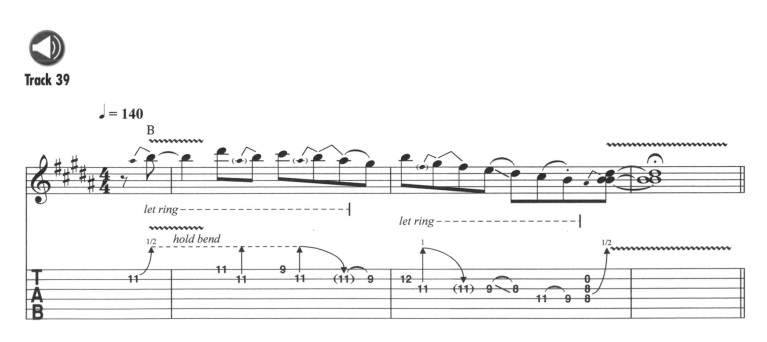

G Major Lick with Open-String Unison Bend

This one has a droning quality faintly reminiscent of a Scottish bagpipe. Begin by bending the D string with your ring finger, and then pull off from your index finger to the open G while the bend is held. Release the bend, pull off, and finish by pushing the D string up to match the open G.

Track 40

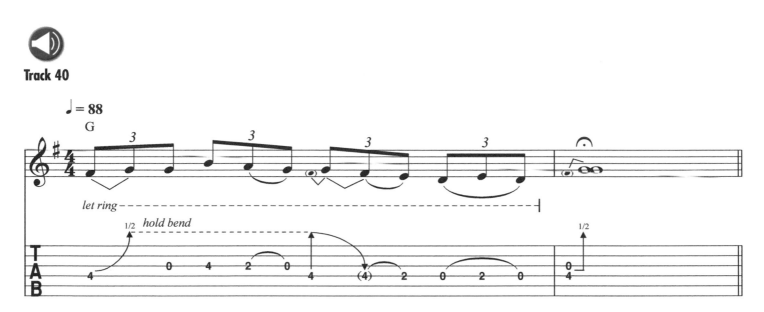

Long G Major Lick

Begin with a ring-finger bend, play the repeated bends in measure 2 with your middle finger, and slide up the D string with your ring finger in the measure that follows.

Track 41

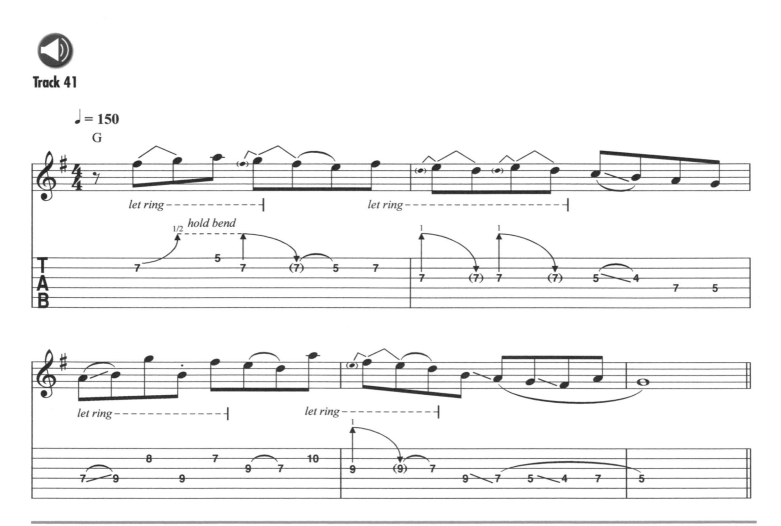

Country/Rock Dominant 7th Lick

Here's a bluesy, rocking lick over E7 that really captures the pedal steel sound if given the proper amount of vibrato. Steel guitar vibrato is rarely wide and exaggerated; rather, it's subtle and controlled, and you need to take that same approach to mimic the left-hand bar workings of a steeler. At the end of measure 2, shift position so you can begin the following measure with an index-finger bend, allowing you to play the final G-string notes with your middle finger.

Track 42

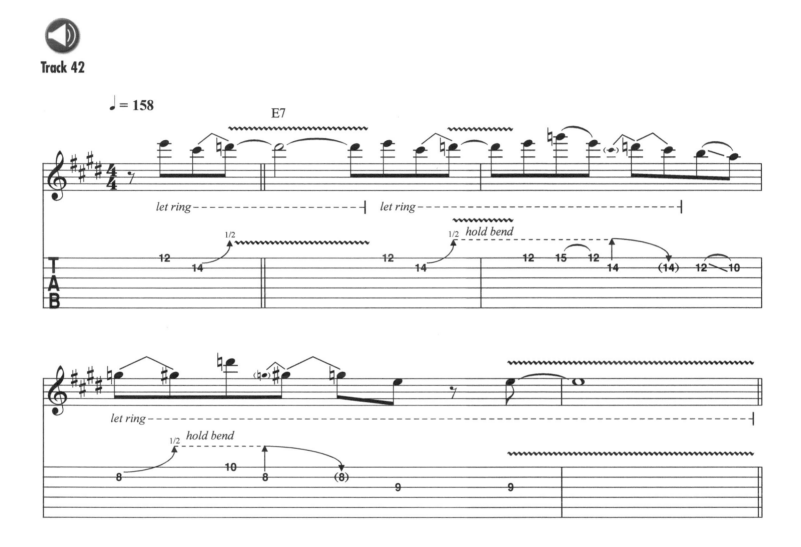

Bending Lick with Open Strings

The open B and high E strings provide a sort of upper pedal or drone during this lick, which has a faintly Beatles-in-their-Indian-phase kind of vibe. The lick contains five prebends, which should be played with your index, ring, middle, ring, and (again) ring fingers, respectively.

Track 43

Behind-the-Nut Bend

This tricky little phrase contains a bend on the headstock-side of the nut—a technique not possible with every guitar, but it's certainly very telecaster-friendly. After a measure of descending eighth notes, use your ring finger and pinky on the first fret of the B and high E strings, respectively, while your index finger bends the open G string up to A (the 3rd of the chord) behind the nut. This one may take some practice, as you'll need to memorize the amount of pressure needed to cleanly bring the string up a whole step. If you miss with these kinds of bends, they sound awful!

Track 44

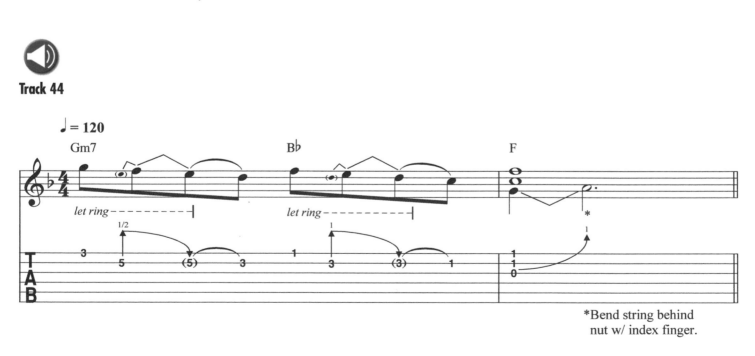

*Bend string behind nut w/ index finger.

Waltzing Melody

Here's a gentle little turnaround in 3/4, fit for use in many of the slow country waltzes in this style. After two measures of bends and releases, wrap up the phase by bending the B string with your index finger and sliding down to the 5th fret; your middle finger should execute the bend on the G string.

Track 45

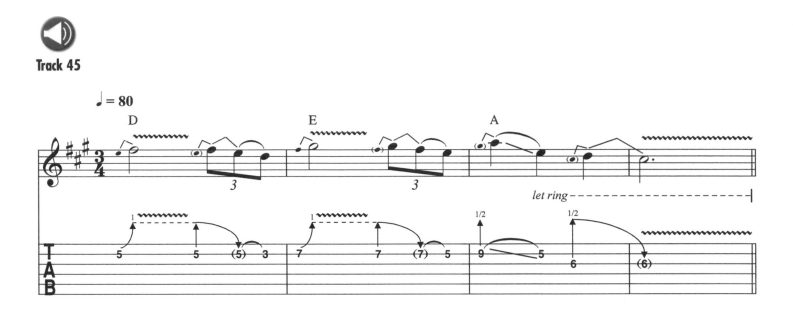

A Major Intro

This is a typical "traditional" country intro in A major. Play the bends in the first two measures with your ring finger while the pinky gets the notes on the high E string. Try playing all of the notes in the next two measures with your index finger alone; the final, pre-bent high A may not be very loud by the time you slide up there, so you may want to give it a little juice with your volume knob or pedal.

Track 46

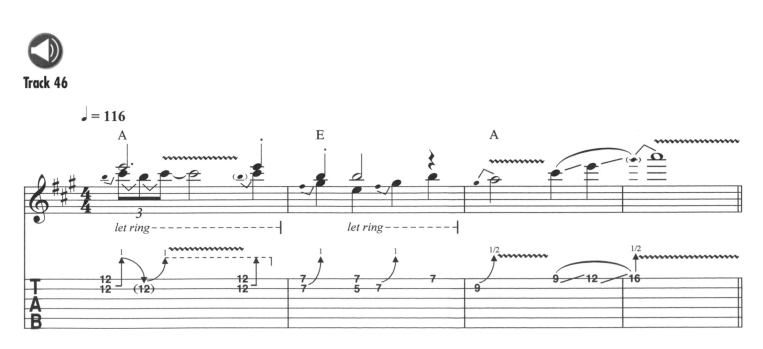

Old-School Intro

This is truly an "old-fashioned" country intro, but one that's still fun to play and full of typical steeler tricks. Begin with your index finger taking care of the two-note pick-up and the first three bends before your ring finger takes over at the 14th fret of the B string. Use your pinky to play the slide from the 12th to the 17th fret on the high E string at the end, and pay particular attention to the "let ring" markings.

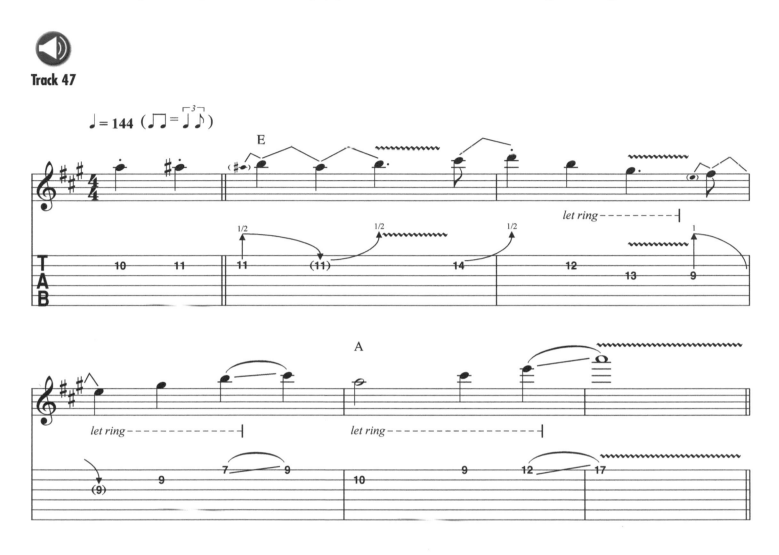

Easy Intro in G Major

Here's another typical country intro, this one featuring multiple bends, each of which should be played with your ring finger while your pinky plays the notes on the string above it. Add some gentle, musical vibrato to mimic the sound of the steeler!

Track 48

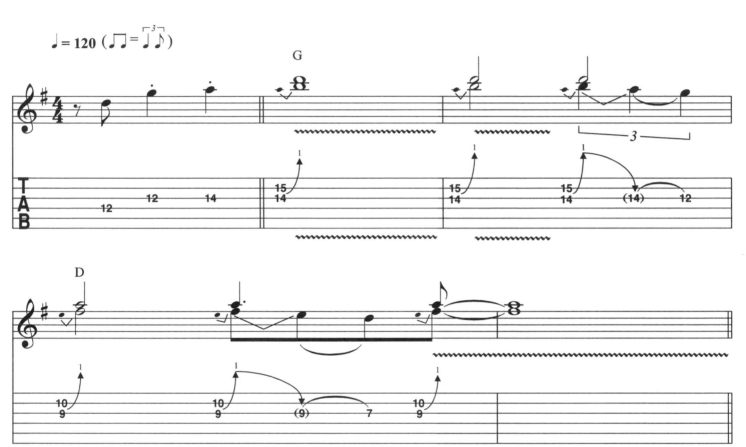

Easy Intro in D Major

The key to this little "trucker's lament" is in the vibrato used to emulate the sound of the steel guitar. After the pick-up, release the B-string bend quickly, à la a grace note. Leave your pinky and ring fingers in place while your index and middle fingers get the notes on the G string. You'll need to use your index finger, with no help from the others, to perform the first bend in the third measure; your middle finger should take care of the D-string bend that follows.

Track 49

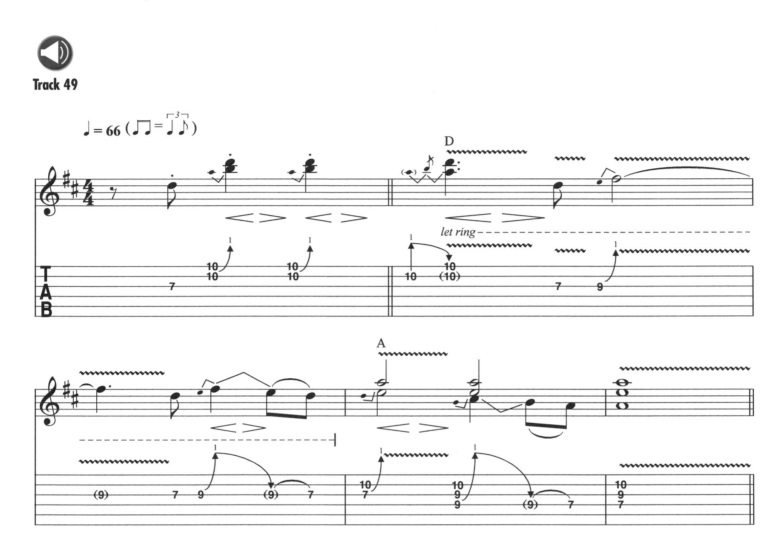

Easy Waltz Intro

This simple little intro in A major contains mostly single notes, leaving you to rely on vibrato and smooth bending to give it that "steely" sound. After two measures of ring-finger bends on the B string, slide down the high E string with your index finger to grab the grace-noted A. Leave your index finger in place, barring the top two strings, and play the bend on the G string with your middle finger

Track 50

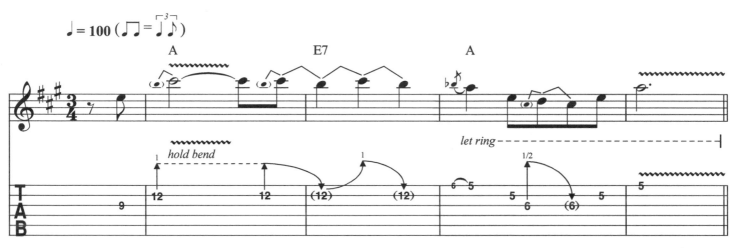

E♭ Major Intro

Introductions are often a steeler's place to shine in country music. Make this one breathe and sing with delicate vibrato and, if you like, subtle use of a volume pedal or knob. Use your index and ring fingers on the G and D strings, respectively, for the sliding double stop in measure 2.

Track 51

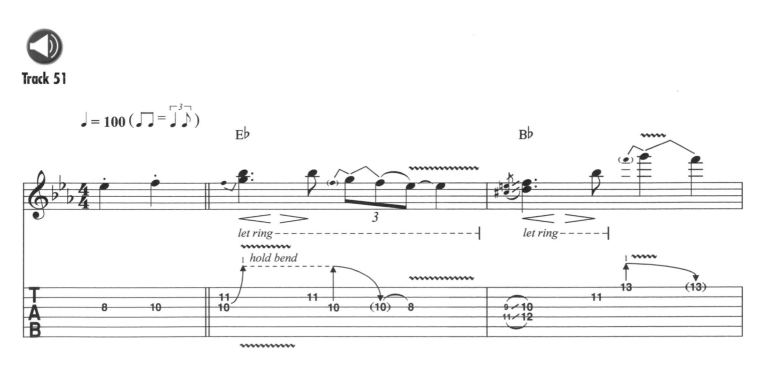

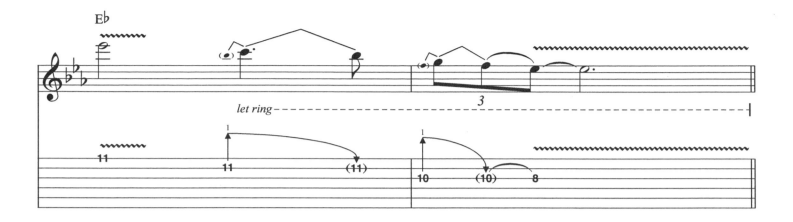

Waltz Progression

This short, gospel-inspired chord sequence is typical of the way a steel guitarist might play during a song's vocal sections, easing back the volume and staying in the background while providing tasty chordal pads for the singer to float above. Use your ring finger for each of the bends except the middle-finger bend in measure 2, and play with a controlled, vocal-like vibrato. Try making up similar two- and three-note background accompaniments to any of your favorite chord progressions, focusing on the more essential chord tones such as 3rds and 7ths. Remember that, in this context, the roots of the chords are always covered by a bassist, keyboardist, or rhythm guitarist, so it's not always essential to include them. Let your ear be your guide!

Track 52

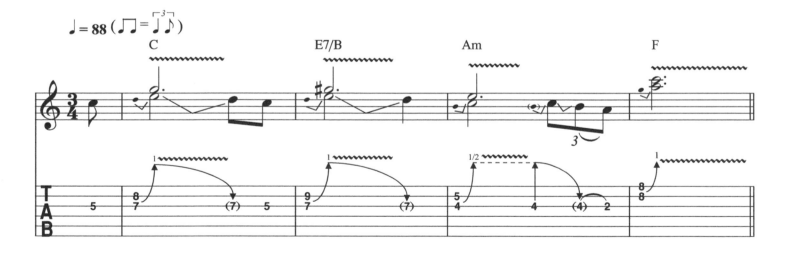

Arpeggiated Progression

While this example is completely atypical of the type of thing a pedal steeler might play (it's rare to hear them do this kind of fingerpicking chordal accompaniment), it does demonstrate another useful application of the prebend-and-release technique. The prebend that begins the example changes the chord from G to Gmaj7. Line up your middle finger behind your pinky on the high E string in order to perform the simultaneous pull-off–and–release that occurs in the example's final measure; make sure to tug a little at the string when you pull-off to make that B sound.

Track 53

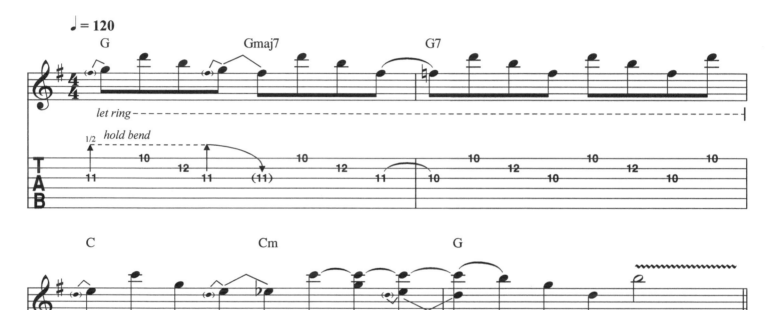

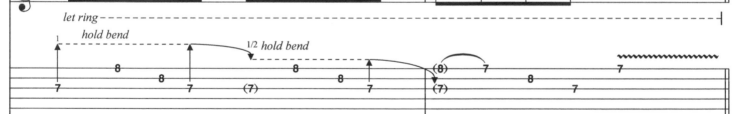

Chord Progression with Pull-Offs and Slides

Here's a short chord sequence that makes use of a handful of essential techniques. Begin with a middle-finger prebend on the G string that's released and pulled off before the B♭ chord becomes a dominant 7th and resolves to E♭. Line up your ring finger behind your pinky on the D string so you can pull off from one to the other, dropping the chord's 3rd a half step and transforming it from major to minor.

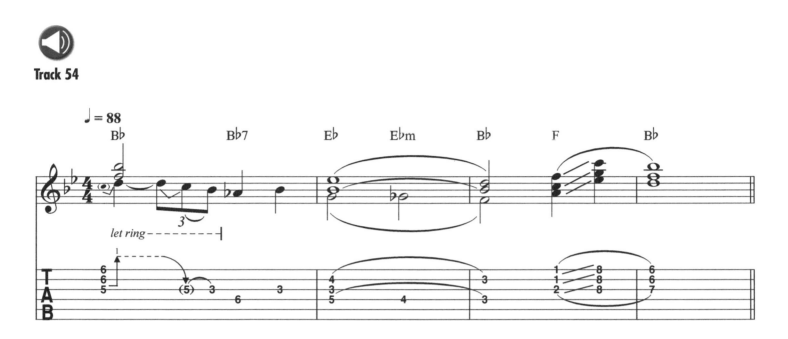

Track 54

Swinging Chords with Slides and Vibrato

This phrase of three-note chords has a bit of Western swing flavor and works well over the first four measures of a G major blues. The trick here is to slide smoothly into the three-note voicings and apply vibrato to the unbent multi-voice chords by repeatedly shaking the hand left and right while firmly holding the chord down—a technique similar to the vibrato used by violinists and players of other fretless stringed instruments.

Track 55

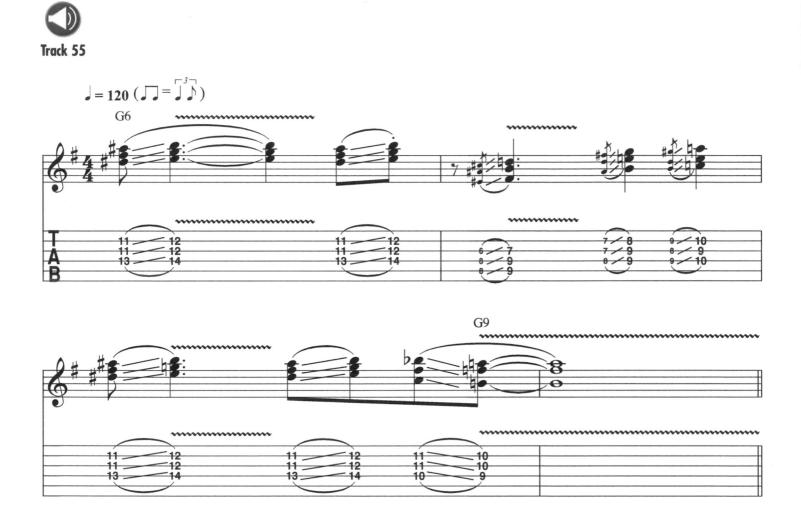

Straight-Eighths Progression

Here's another familiar chord progression. Play the G-string bends in measure 3 with your index finger, rolling it down to quickly grab the note on the D string while your pinky and middle fingers remain in place on the B and high E strings.

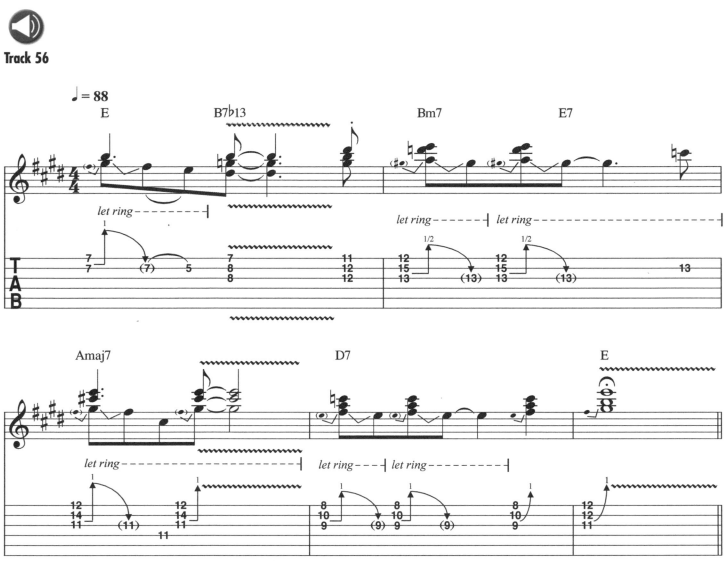

Bends in Two Octaves

This simple lick jumps back and forth between G and C chords, relying on ring-finger bends throughout. You'll need to acclimate yourself to the differing strengths needed to execute the C major bends in both the upper and lower registers. Notice, too, the ghost notes—those are common in "chicken pickin'" during position shifts.

Track 57

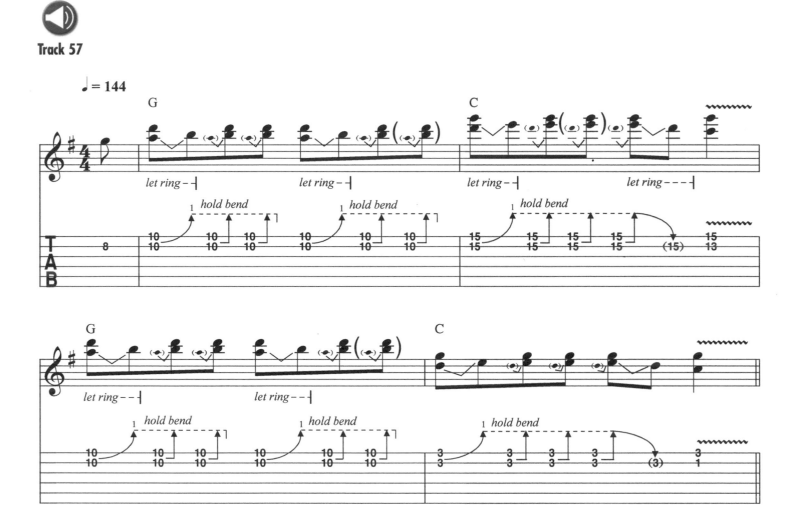

Chromatic Passing Chords

This short progression in 6ths merely hints at the possible uses for chromatic passing chords that connect one diatonic chord to another. Keep in mind that this book is not merely a collection of licks and fragments that imitate the sound of pedal steel, but also a guide containing techniques designed to help you to create steel guitar sounds of your own. Look for spots in your music where you can use these tasty chromatic tidbits—you're limited only by the scope of your imagination!

Track 58

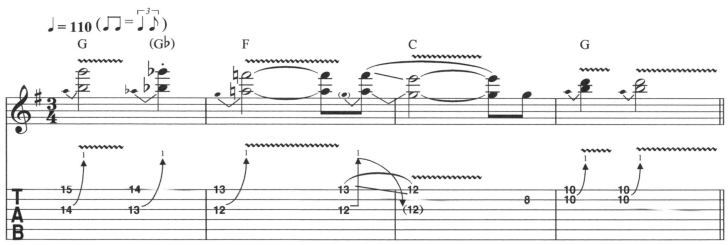

Progression with Secondary Dominants

Secondary dominants occur when "normal" diatonic chords (in this case, C♯ and F♯) are converted to dominants, thus creating a resolution to non-tonic chords. In this case, C♯ becomes the V of ii, F♯, and F♯ becomes the V of V, B. It's a device common to all musical styles, but particularly prevalent in country and jazz idioms. The D chord here serves as a chromatic passing chord before the C♯ and the II–V–I turnaround. Use your ring finger on the B string and your middle on the D string for the lick's final double stop.

Track 59

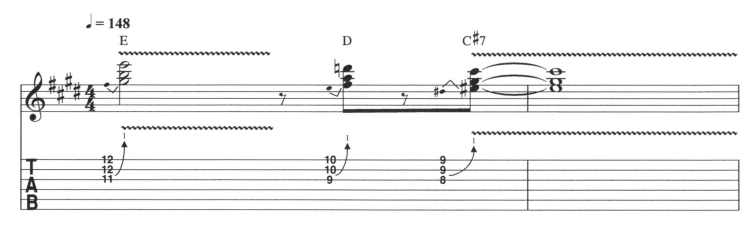

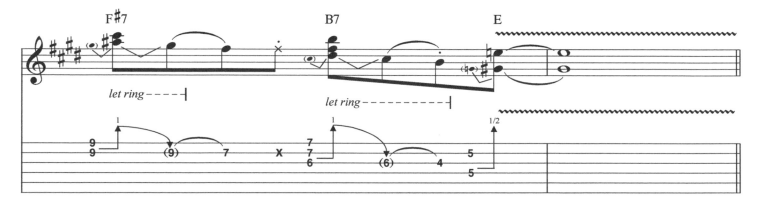

45

Country/Rock Bends

This is a classic steeler's lick for any bluesy, dominant chord situation. Use your pinky on the high E string throughout, with your middle finger executing the B-string bends and your ring finger grabbing the notes on the G string. Strong vibrato on the held bent notes really captures the sound of steel!

Track 60

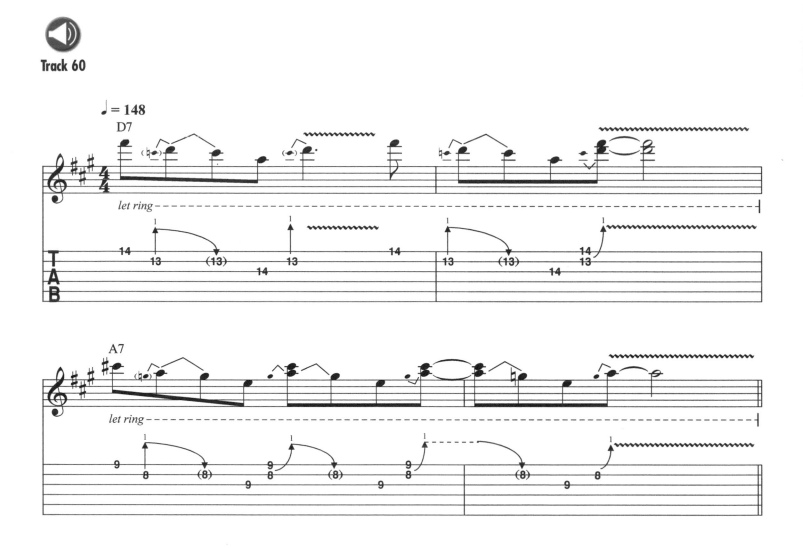

Behind-the-Nut Bend in B♭

Here's another lick featuring bending on the headstock side of the nut; note that this may not be possible on all guitars. This one is challenging; the open G string must be pushed up a step and a half to B♭ and then lowered a whole step to A♭, all with the index finger applying pressure behind the nut. If you can pull this one off on your guitar, you may find it isn't easy to get these types of bends in tune. You have to memorize the exact amount of finger pressure needed to raise and lower the open string accurately.

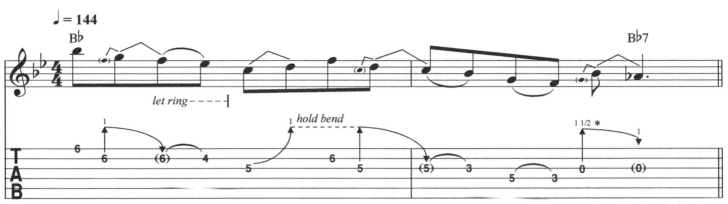

Bend string behind nut.

Behind-the-Nut Suspension-and-Release Lick

This lick further illustrates the possibilities of behind-the-nut bending. After a familiar sequence of ring-finger prebend-and-release figures, grab the top three open strings and use your index finger to push the G string up a whole step behind the nut and then lower it a half step, creating a suspension-and-release in E major. This one should be a lot easier than the previous example, as you're raising the string only a whole step this time and have the open B and high E strings to use as guides for intonation.

Track 62

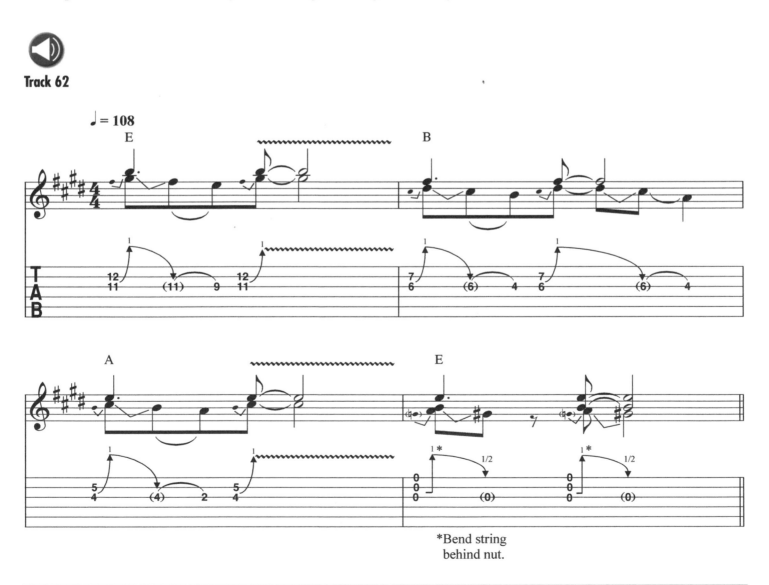

*Bend string
behind nut.*

Double Stop Lick with Ascending Major Chords

This lick combines typical B-string bending (but no Parsons/White B-Benders for us, thank you!) with an unusual turnaround. The phrase, with ring-finger bends throughout, is in G major but borrows the E♭ and F major chords from the parallel minor key, G minor.

Track 63

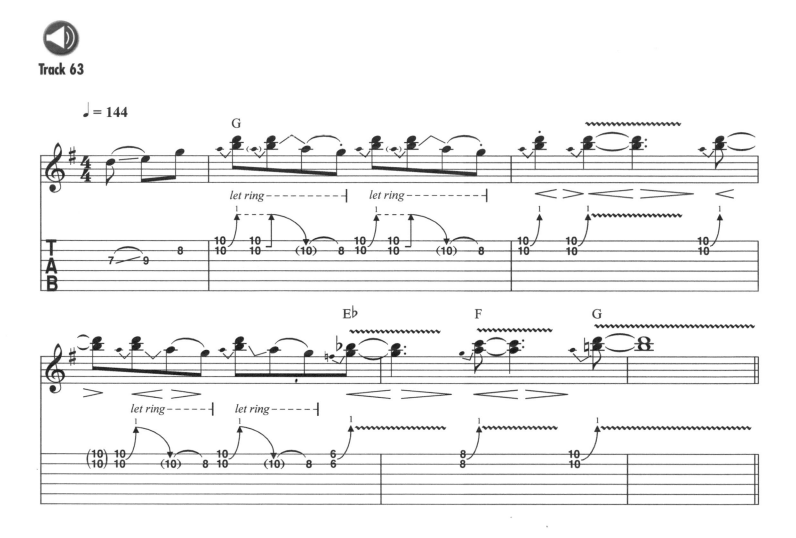

Held-Bend Lick in B♭

Here's another lick that takes you to the key of the IV chord, E♭, and it's minor incarnation before wending its way back to the tonic. Use your ring finger to bend and hold the B string in the first measure, and then bend the G string with your middle finger, holding it fast while you play the notes on the strings above it. Play the remaining bends with your ring finger, taking care to get both the whole and half step bends in tune before applying vibrato.

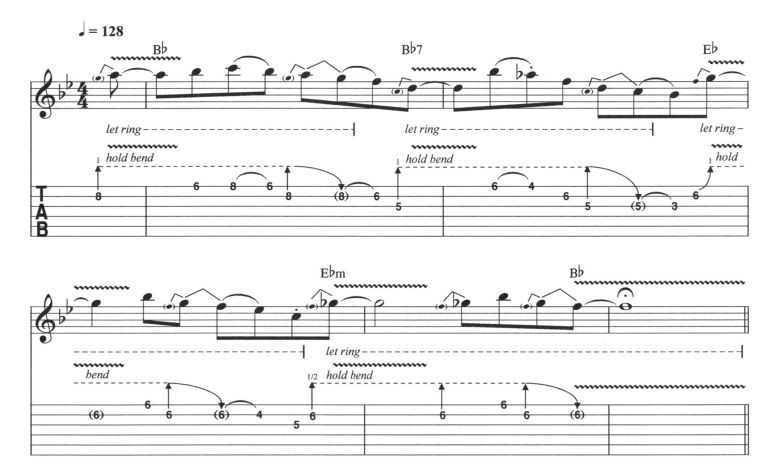

Waltz Lick with Chromatic Passing Chord

This simple sequence in A♭ includes a chromatic passing chord (D) that bridges the gap between the V and IV chords. Play the quick chromatic triplet here with your ring finger on the B string and your middle finger on the G string to execute the bend-and-release figure, and then slide the shape down for the D♭ figure that follows.

Track 65

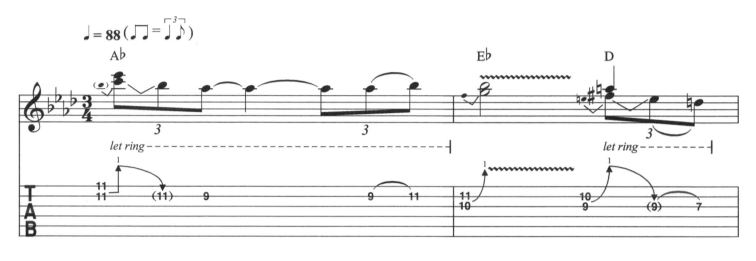

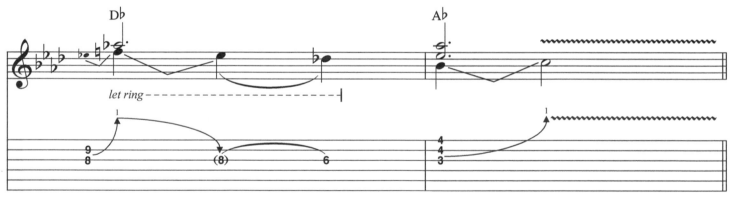

IV–I Lick in E♭ Major

This long, flowing eighth note line is typical of the single-line solos steelers play on medium and up-tempo tunes. Begin with your pinky playing the pick-up on the high E string and leave it there until the halfway point of the third measure. Execute the G-string prebend in measure 2 with your middle finger while your index finger remains on the B string, creating a nice minor 2nd rub.

Track 66

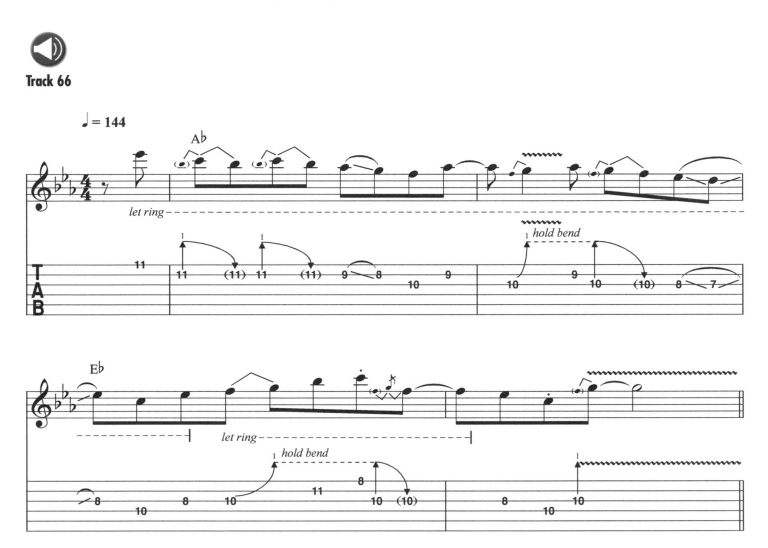

Blues Turnaround

For this turnaround in A, use your index and ring fingers on the high E and B strings, respectively, while your middle finger prebends and releases the G string during the first two measures. In measure 3, leave your pinky in place on the B string while your ring finger bends and releases the G string and then pulls off to your index finger. The final eighth notes should be played with your middle finger.

Track 67

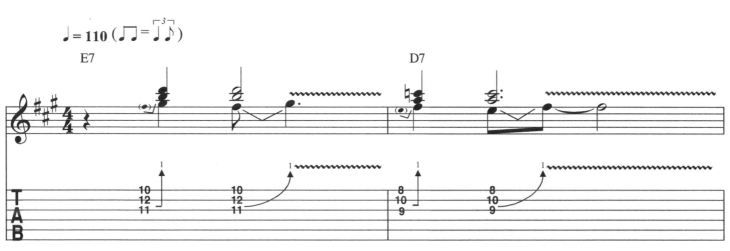

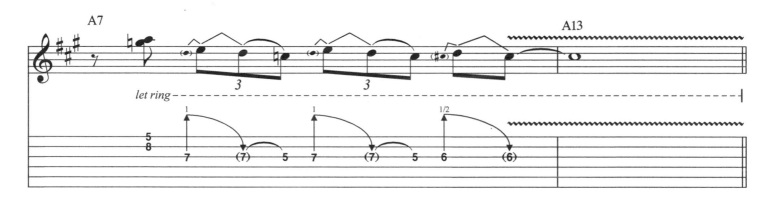

Bluesy Phrase in G Major

Begin this set of dominant chord ideas by pulling off from your ring to your index finger on the high E string, executing the G-string bend with your middle finger. Move the phrase down a whole step over the F7 chord, and then finish with your pinky on the high E string and your middle finger bending and releasing the B string in measure 3. Play the final G-string bend-and-release with your ring finger, and then pull off to your index finger and complete the phrase.

Track 68

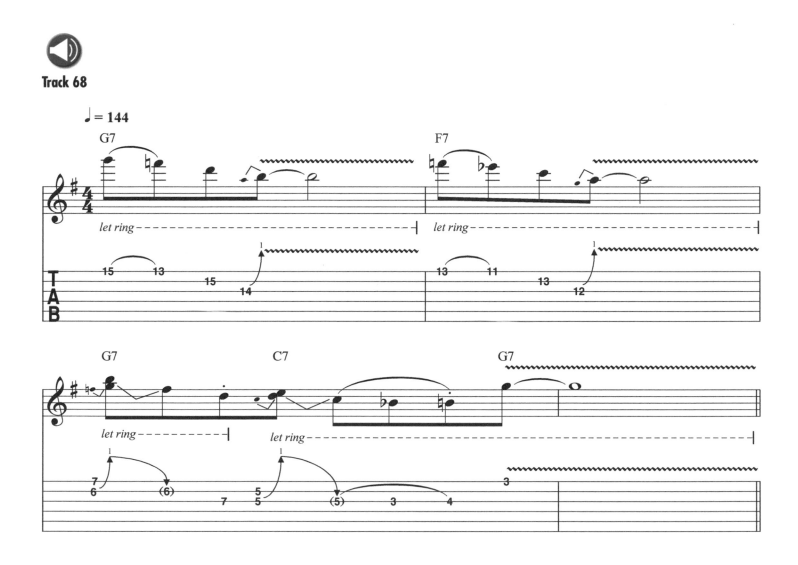

Short Ballad Break

Playing slow ballad solos like the short example below requires special care. The bends are held longer and precise intonation—or the lack of it—can really come to the fore. The two bends in measure 1 should be played with your middle finger, while the ring finger grabs the Ds on the high E string. The pre-bent G string in measure 2 requires a quick shift of hand position to allow your ring finger to do the work, before shifting again to 10th position for measure 3. Use your middle finger for the final suspension-and-release bends on the G string.

Track 69

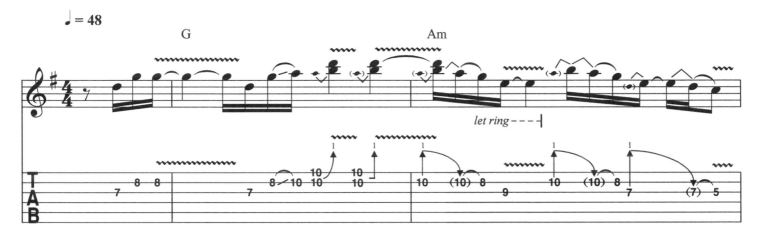

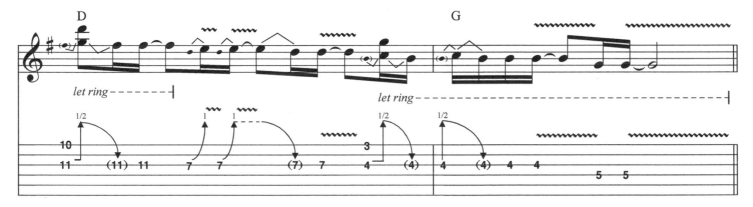

Fast Lick in C Major

This four-measure phrase strings a number of earlier licks together into one long eighth note line that requires a bit of shifting on the fly to execute smoothly. Begin with a ring-finger bend on the B string and end the first measure with your middle finger bending the G string up a whole step. Play the B-string bend in measure 3 with your middle finger, and the final G-string bend with your ring finger while your pinky remains anchored above it.

Track 70

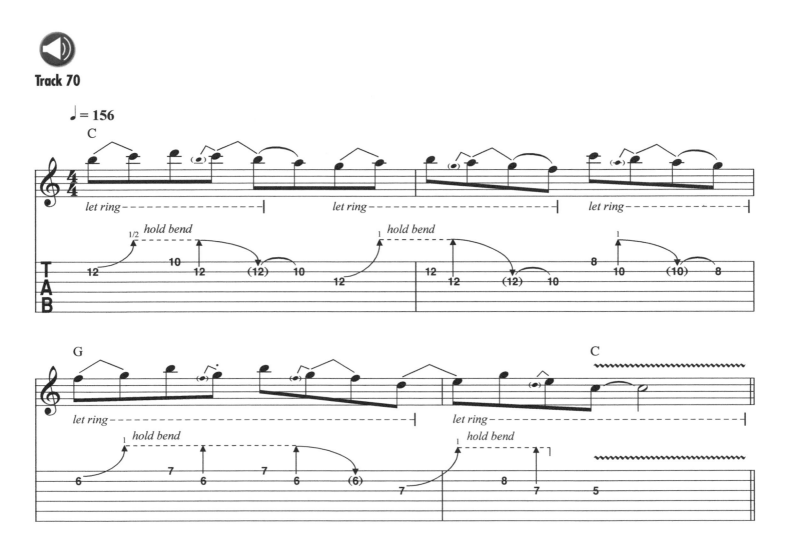

D Major Phrase

Here's another long, flowing eighth note lick that gives you a chance to put together previous ideas and techniques. Get it started with your ring finger bending the B string and your pinky on the high E above it; follow by sliding your index finger down the B string from the 12th to the 10th fret while your middle finger bends the G string and holds it. Measure 2 will find you holding the bent G string while your index finger gets to the B string and your pinky grabs the F♯ on the 14th fret of the high E. You're then in perfect position to slide your ring finger down the high E string from the 12th to the 10th fret, leaving it anchored there until the end of the phrase.

Track 71

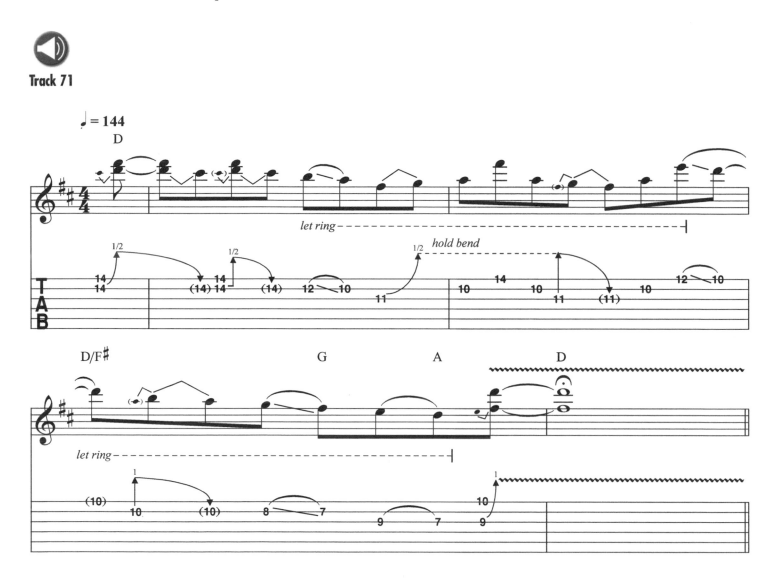

Bent and Sliding 6ths

Steel guitarists play a lot of sliding and shifting 6ths licks and they're a whole lot easier to pull off with pedals and levers than with the multiple prebends we're stuck with! Be patient—don't worry about speed at first, as that will come with time—rushing will only sacrifice pitch accuracy and technique that must be built up slowly. Begin this phrase with your ring finger on the high E string and middle finger bending the G string, and then slide your hand down and shift, using your index finger to nail the D that begins the second measure. The whole process is then essentially repeated, with the middle finger bending D to E with the ring finger above it, and then shifting to execute the final bend with the index finger above.

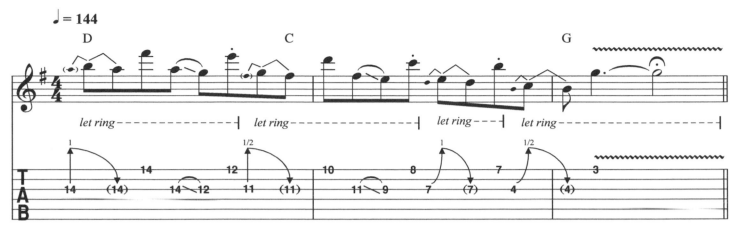

E Major Phrase

This sunny little lick begins with your index finger at the 12th fret of the high E string while your ring finger bends the B string below it. Use your index finger to slide down to the 9th fret and then follow with a middle-finger unison bend on the G string—watch that intonation! The G- and B-string bends in the third measure should be taken by your middle and ring fingers, respectively.

Track 73

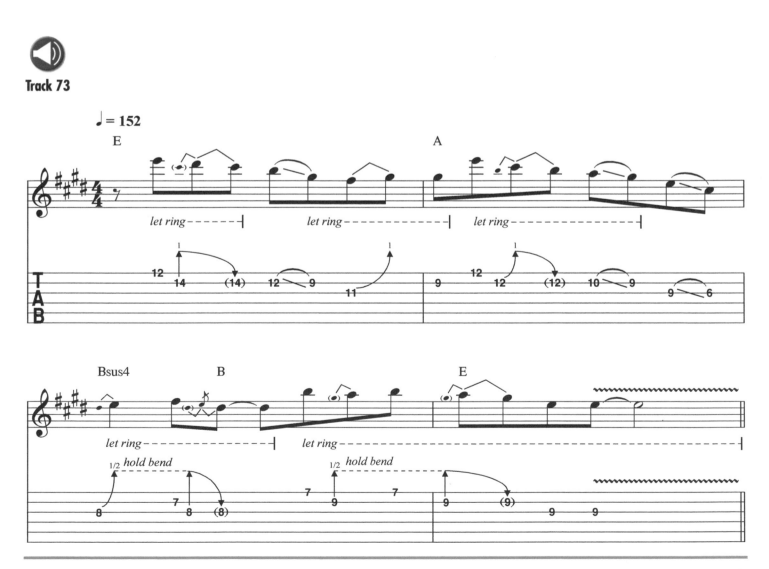

Rapid-Fire 6ths #1

While the target speed of this lick is "rapid fire," you'll nevertheless have to begin slowly and work it up to speed—fast and sloppy is never good. Begin with a G-string hammer-on from your index to your middle finger, and then grab the G on the high E string with your index finger. Follow by sliding your middle and ring fingers up the G and high E strings, respectively, in a line of ascending 6ths. The second half of the lick jumps up the fingerboard quickly, with your pinky on the E string at the beginning of measure 3 and your middle finger executing the B-string prebend-and-release. Use the same fingering for the second set of eighth notes in this measure, shifting your hand down so that your pinky plays the E.

Track 74

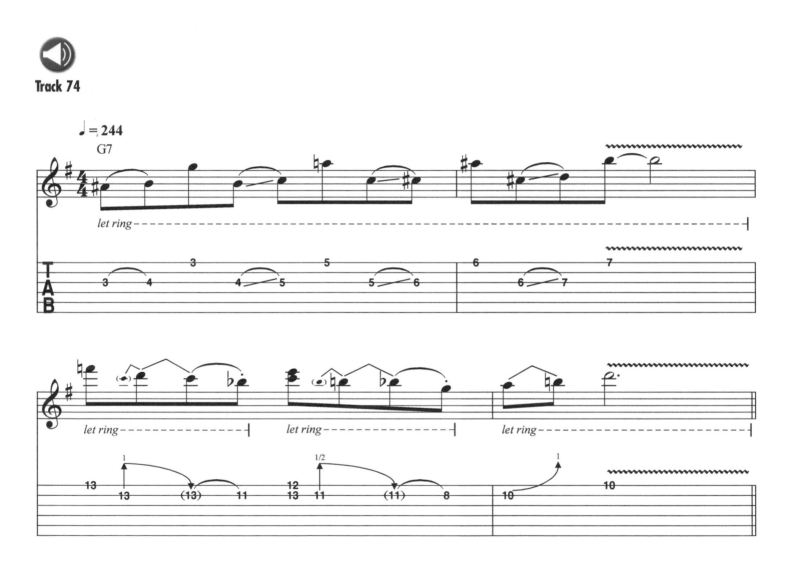

Rapid-Fire 6ths #2

As with the previous example, be patient and work this one up slowly. Measure 1 contains familiar sliding 6ths and a final "chicken-picked" eighth note that allows you to shift your hand quickly to 8th position for the line that follows—a held, ring-finger, B-string bend and subsequent notes on the high E string. For the final two measures, leave your ring finger and pinky in place on the B and high E strings until the last two notes—your index and middle fingers can take care of the rest.

Track 75

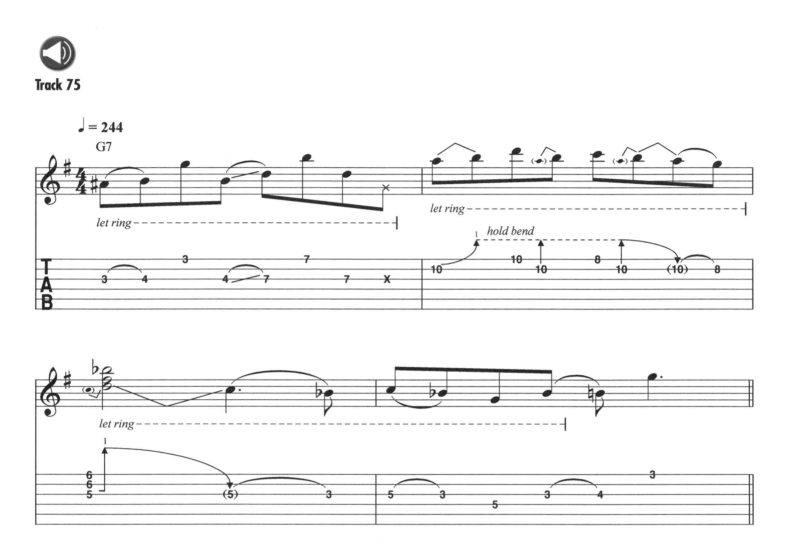

Longer Licks and Phrases

The examples that follow are longer and more involved, and incorporate elements of what we've learned so far with an eye towards a melodic, musical application of faux-steel techniques. Ideally, your efforts should begin to sound less like a series of strung-together licks and more like a natural and cohesive extension of your own unique playing style.

C Major Phrase with Chromatic Passing Chords

Begin this phrase with a middle-finger bend, which will set you in position for the second measure; use your ring finger and pinky for the notes on the top two strings, followed by a quick shift allowing your pinky to grab the high E on beat 3. The third measure features chromatically descending double stops—use your ring finger and pinky here—that wind their way down to D. After all of the B-string bending be sure to get those final G-string bends in tune—don't overbend to compensate for the heavier string!

Track 76

Country/Rock Intro

This melodic, medium-tempo intro is packed with typical steel moves. After the pick-up, use your ring finger for all of the B-string bends in the first three measures. You'll need to use your middle finger for the prebend-and-release figure in measure 4, leaving your index finger stationary on the high E string. From there, it's all ring-finger bends until the final descending pattern that ends the phrase.

Track 77

A Major Phrase with Secondary Dominants

This nearly full-length solo in A major begins with a middle finger slide up the G string. After the double bar, bend the B string and hold it with your middle finger while your ring finger and pinky get to work on the high E string. There are two unsupported index-finger bends near the end—the first occurs when the B string is pushed up a half step to become the 3rd of the F#7 chord, and the second when you bend into the tonic on the example's final chord.

Track 78

Uptempo Break in G Major

This fun phrase begins on the IV chord in G major and combines single lines, double stops, and three-note chords to give you a little taste of everything. After beginning with some familiar G-string, ring-finger bend-and-releases figures, climb the neck and ape the opening idea over the tonic chord. You'll need to use your middle finger for the G-string bend (pick-up to measure 3); this will allow you to slide from the 12th to the 16th fret with your index finger, putting you in position to execute the double stops with your index and middle fingers. Use a ring-finger barre for the sliding chords that follow (where possible) and be careful not to cut your fingers—you'll need to slide and press down very firmly to hear each chord tone (particularly in the hammer-ons).

Track 79

Country/Jazz Progression

This short, melodic break is based on chord movement commonly encountered in jazz, R&B, and more contemporary country styles. Begin with a ring-finger bend-and-hold before shifting positions to execute the same bend with your middle finger in measure 2; use your pinky to play the 3rd of the G#7 chord on the high E string. Play the G-string bend in the fourth measure with your ring finger, as this will allow your pinky to grab the D♮ on the B string.

Track 80

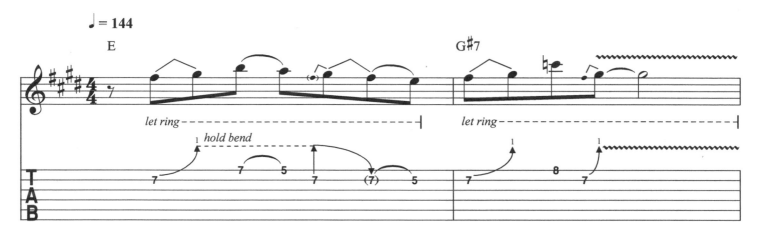

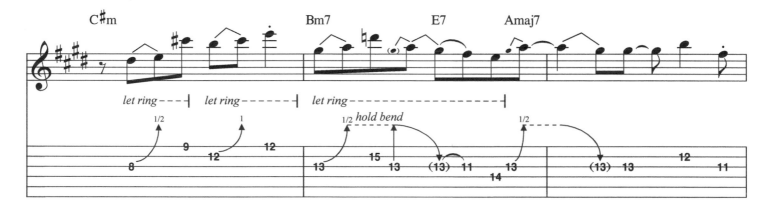

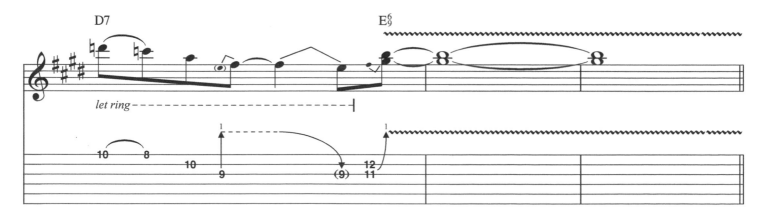

Bb Major Progression

Here's another typical chord sequence with a relaxed, medium-tempo approach. Play the repeated B-string bends in the first three measures with your ring finger before using your index finger for the bends over E°7. The second half of the example is made up of sliding double stops in 6ths and a quick V–IV–I turnaround, including a slide down the B string with your index finger at the very end.

Track 81

65

Banjo Roll–Style Lick

Steel guitarists often employ a device taken from banjo technique in which two notes on different strings are played in rapid succession by rolling back and forth between the right-hand thumb and index finger repeatedly. Players of both instruments usually wear metal fingerpicks, but you can try this lick with either bare fingers or a standard flatpick. Here, you're working primarily between the B and high E strings and employing ring-finger bending exclusively. Work this one up to speed slowly and then watch out—it's a gas when you can fire off these kinds of licks at machine-gun speeds.

Track 82

Vibrating Arpeggios

These "vibrating arpeggios" are more stylistically typical of blues guitar than steel, but it's a technique that's occasionally encountered in both pedal and lap steel as well. The aim here is to mimic the shaking of the left-hand bar by employing a healthy dose of vibrato to each chord as it passes. Because we're not bending strings here (until the very end), the vibrato must be applied by a repeated shaking of the fretting hand from the left to the right with as much force and speed as you can muster while keeping the chord forms intact and on the neck. The faster and heavier you lay it on, the less it will sound like guitar and the more you'll be "copping the bar"! It *is* possible to use "up and down" vibrato in this situation, but be sure to press down firmly and try not to detune the chord altogether. The rootless chords that make up this example are modeled after the chord style of steel guitarists. They rarely play large voicings in a band context, and their pedals and knee levers allow for smooth voice leading that moves in small intervals as opposed to the jumpier "grips" that guitar players move around the neck.

Track 83

Slow Country/Blues Progression in G Major

Here's a triplet-laden example with an old-fashioned feel and a variety of steeler's tricks. After the opening bend, use your pinky to slide up the high E string and back down again, holding the B that rings throughout the second measure while your index finger executes the prebend-and-release below it. A series of triplets over E7 follow, beginning with the held ring-finger bend on the B string that releases and then works itself down the neck. Following a IV–V turnaround, there's a return to the tonic chord and a bit of middle-finger G-string bending before ending on a G6 chord approached chromatically from below.

Track 84

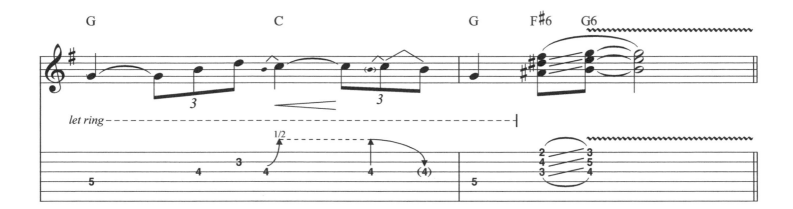

Ballad Waltz Intro

This straightforward-sounding intro is actually packed with a number of challenging techniques. After the pick-up, use your ring finger to bend the G string up a whole step while your pinky takes care of the B string and your index finger—stretch now!—lands on the 1st fret of the high E string. Keep your fingers in place until you release into measure 3, which ends with an unsupported index-finger bend on the B string. After a simple turnaround, the example finishes with a double stop over a C7 chord; use your index finger to bend the B string up a half step behind the nut.

Track 85

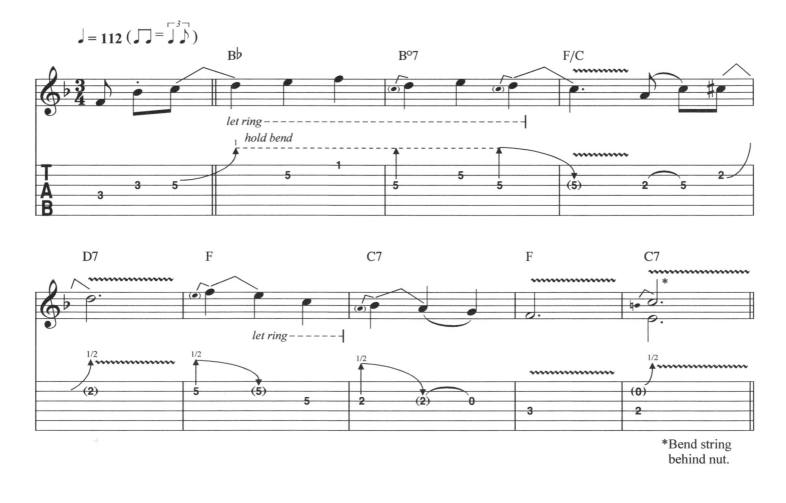

Ballad Accompaniment

This next example mimics a steeler's approach to chordal accompaniment in a country/rock ballad style. The playing is generally spacious and unobtrusive, providing ambience and textured pads of sound over which the rest of the band can do their thing. Go for a smooth sound and a legato approach with carefully applied vibrato and attention to the "let ring" markings. Remember that ballad settings provide the most time and space to expose any deficiencies of technique and intonation!

Track 86

Swinging Turnaround with Whole Tone Pattern

This one mixes down-home country flavor with a touch of bebop and swing and combines single lines, double stops, and rootless chords. Play the first two bends with your middle finger; your index and middle fingers should handle the sliding D#°7 double stops. After the tonic chord in measure 3, there's a quick sequence of secondary dominants in rootless voicings followed by a turnaround containing a familiar lick over B7 and a whole note pattern of descending augmented chords—a cherished steeler's device—based on an E9♭13 chord. The half step bend on the high E string in measure 7 should be played with your pinky.

Track 87

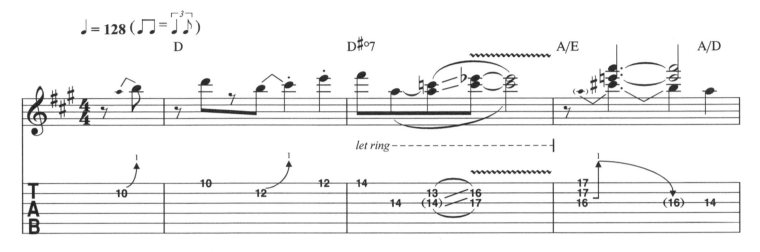

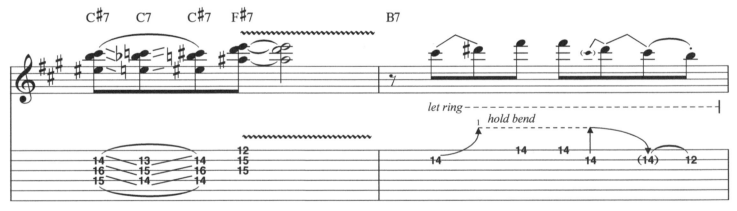

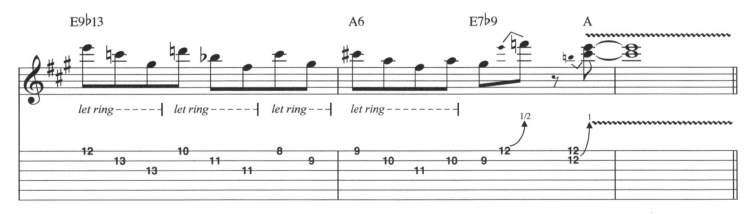

Country/Rock Break in G Major

This fun, rollicking phrase contains no surprises but assembles a handful of earlier licks into a strong emulation of a pedal steel solo spot. Use your pinky on the high E string and your middle finger for the B-string bends in the first four measures. The unusual D7–E7–F7 turnaround features ring-finger prebend-and-releases along the B string before the example closes with your index finger on the high E string and your ring finger bending the B string up and down.

Track 88

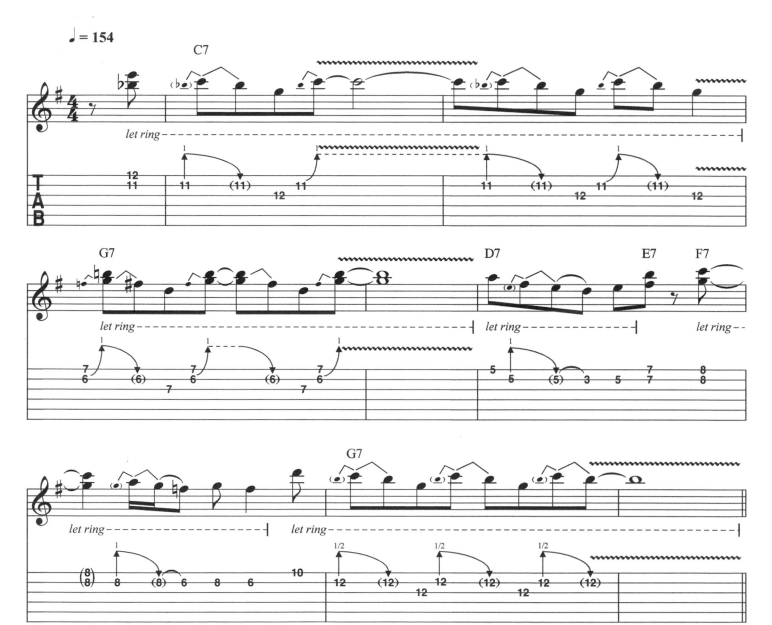

Complete Solos

The solos that follow—all based on commonly encountered country and rock chord progressions—are designed to give the fledgling pedal steel emulator a look at how the elements examined so far can be assembled into cohesive, musical statements and used in soloing applications. Based on both previously encountered licks and new material, these solos should serve as guides toward composing your own faux-steel outings and, ultimately, fully improvised solo spots in the style.

Country/Rock Solo in C Major

This 16-measure solo is based on typical country and rock chord changes and features mostly single, eighth note lines broken up by the occasional double stop. Begin with your ring finger and pinky on the B and high E strings, respectively, while your middle finger executes the bend-and-hold on the G string. Use your index finger to get to the A in measure 2, and then to back up your middle finger to play the difficult D-string bend in measure 3. After some tasty double stop bends over Am, G, and F, there's an unsupported index-finger bend in measure 7. Measures 8 and 9 are mirrored in the two measures that follow, each time containing a ghosted or chicken-picked note that allows you to shift into position for the following measure. The final four measures begin with a middle-finger bend on the G string while your index finger barres the top two strings at the 8th fret.

Track 89

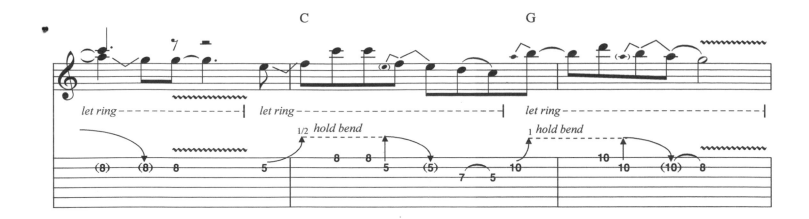

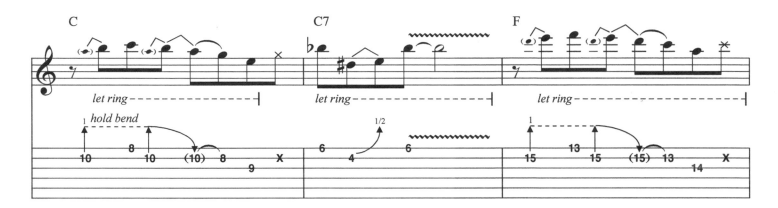

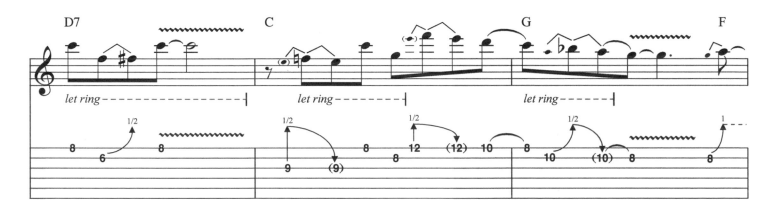

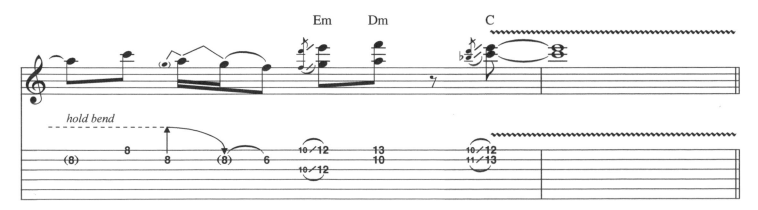

Country/Rock Solo in F Major

This melodic eight-measure solo focuses on the potential for single-line soloing in the pedal steel style, with held and ringing bends across two strings. The first three prebends should be played with the ring finger; take the fourth, a bend-and-release over a C7 chord at the end of measure 3, with your middle finger. The bends over the Bb chord should likewise be played with the ring finger—sound familiar?—before the solo ends with a combination of bent notes and melodic double stops.

Track 90

Simple Country Solo in C Major

This basic and straightforward solo puts some of the easier licks you've learned into context over simple chord changes that are encountered in many country and rock songs. If you've worked your way through this book, there will be little that's unfamiliar at this point. The challenge here is in a few quick shifts of position and in the execution of the material in a musical and dynamic way.

Track 91

E Major Solo with Combined Techniques

This pretty solo, built around simple chords and a classic, old school rock 'n' roll groove, combines techniques such as oblique bends, multi-string phrases, and open-string unisons into a coherent musical statement. Begin by bending the D string with your ring finger and holding it for the first of the three triplets. Play the triplets in measure 3 by pulling off from your ring finger to your index finger on the high E string and using your ring finger and pinky on the B and G strings, respectively. Take the first prebend over the A chord with your ring finger, and the second with your middle finger; repeat the procedure with the B chord that follows. For the final two measures, let the open high E string ring while your ring finger and pinky do the work on the B string, and your middle finger bends, releases, and re-bends the G string, matching the open string above.

Track 92

Slow Gospel/Jazz Solo in A

This relaxed but complex solo in 6/8 combines the influences of jazz, gospel, and country, and explores a variety of techniques, not least of which is the way in which steel guitarists superimpose augmented and diminished triads over dominant 7th chords. The first of these occurs in measure 2, where sliding double stops (played by the index and middle fingers) create an augmented sound on an E7 chord, echoed later in the penultimate measure as three-note augmented voicings resolving back to the tonic. Measures 3 and 4 feature repeated middle-finger bends while the index and ring fingers remain stationary on the strings above; play the ascending E–E♯–F♯ in measures 7–8 with your pinky on the high E string.

Track 93

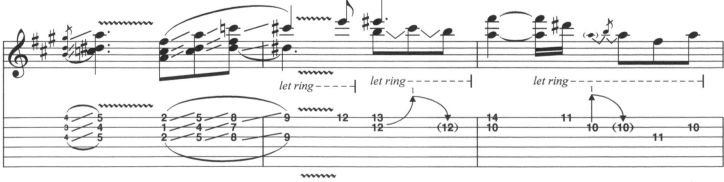

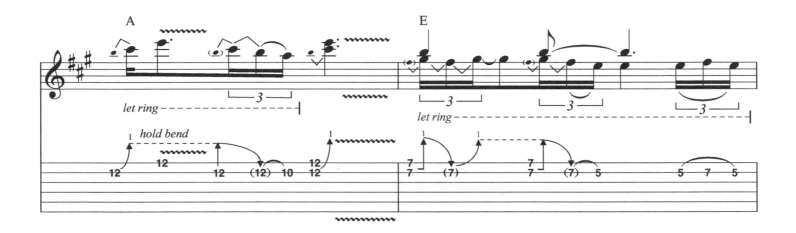

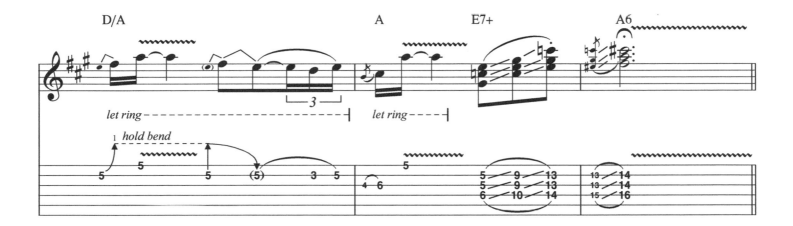

Ballad Solo in E♭ Major

Here's a pretty ballad break with a lot of space to add tasty vibrato and a little volume pedal work if the mood strikes you. The example begins with a two-string harmony bend on the G and B strings (use your ring and middle fingers, respectively) that's held and gently shaken before being released. Bend into the unison in measure 3 with your pinky and watch the pitch—sloppy intonation will really stand out here. Roll quickly between your thumb and index finger for the G and high E double stops in the final measure, creating a tremolo-like effect.

Track 94

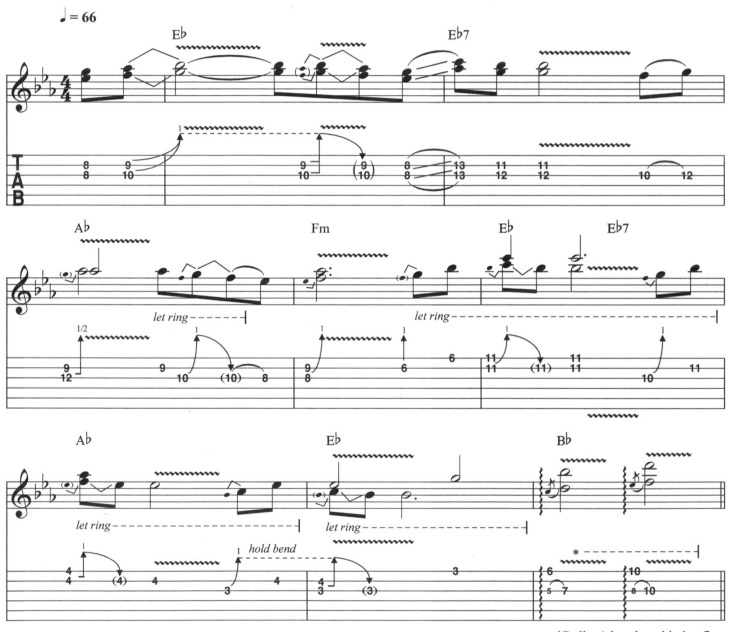

*Roll w/ thumb and index finger
as quickly as possible.

Ballad Solo in D Major with Sliding Augmented Chords

This medium tempo ballad solo should be played with a cut time feel and includes more of the sliding augmented chords encountered earlier. After the pick-up, bend the G string with your ring finger, allowing your pinky and index finger to play the notes on the B and high E strings in the measures that follow. Play the G in measure 3 (8th fret of the B string) with your index finger and follow with a middle-finger prebend-and-release. The augmented chords in measure 6 should be played with your index finger barring the G and B strings and your middle finger on the D string. In the final measure, use your index finger on the high E string while your middle and ring fingers get to the notes on the G and B strings, respectively.

Track 95

Ballad Solo in E Major

Here's another simple, beautiful ballad break, typical of the spacious, melodic playing steelers often do in this type of setting. Use your middle finger for the sliding pick-up, and then follow with your ring and index fingers on the B and high E strings, respectively. Shift positions in measure 3 so that your index finger is on the B string and your middle finger takes care of the pitches on the G string during the quarter note triplet and in the measure that follows. Play the bend in measure 6 with your ring finger—this will allow you to slide into the double stop in the next measure. Use that same finger for the 16th note bends at the end.

Track 96

Blues Solo in A Major

Yes, even steelers get the blues. In this first of three 12-bar blues solos, let's examine how the licks you've learned so far can be applied in a blues context. Begin with a ring-finger bend that's held as you get to work on the high E string; the bend is then released and followed by G-string bending performed by the middle finger. Use an index-finger barre (4th fret) in measure 6 before sliding up a fret and spinning off a classic blues lick over the tonic chord. The held bend in measure 11 should be played with the ring finger; this will allow you to grab the As (G string, 14th fret) that follow with your middle finger.

Track 97

Blues Solo in E Major

This second blues solo is in the key of E major and also features primarily single-line licks peppered with the occasional double stop. Begin by bending the B string with your middle finger; take the notes on the high E string with your pinky and the subsequent G-string bends with your index finger. Play the B-string bend-and-releases toward the end in measure 11 with your ring finger, and use the pinky to get to the notes on the high E string.

Track 98

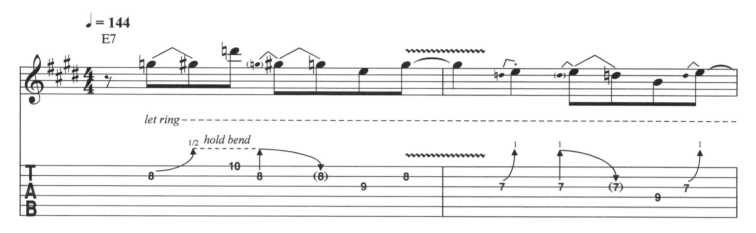

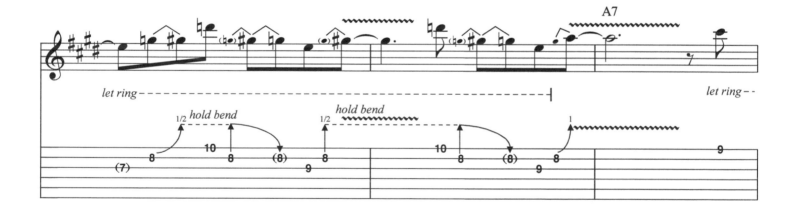

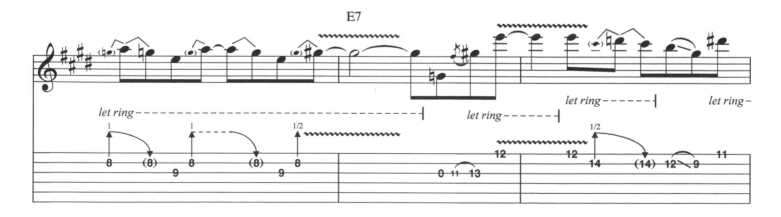

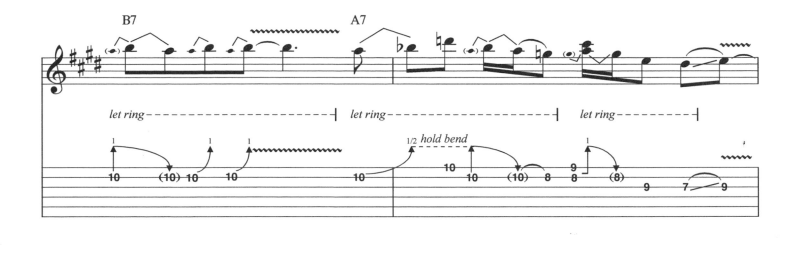

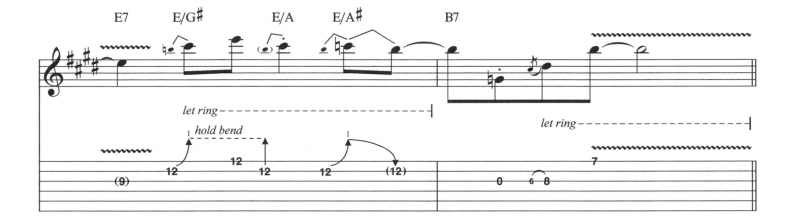

Swinging Blues Chord Solo in C Major

This final solo is comprised of three-note chords that should really put your multi-string vibrato technique to the test. In situations such as these where no string bending occurs, you can mimic the sound of pedal steel with strong chordal vibrato and lots of smooth sliding from voicing to voicing. Push down firmly with your fretting hand as you slide chords to be sure that each voice can be heard. Carefully observe each grace note, vibrato, and slide marking, and don't miss the sprinkling of passing diminished and augmented chords.

Track 99

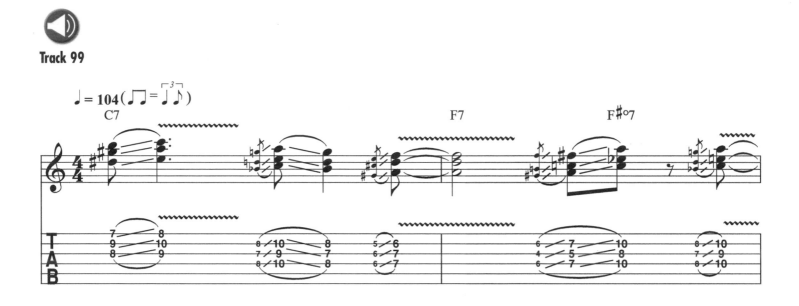

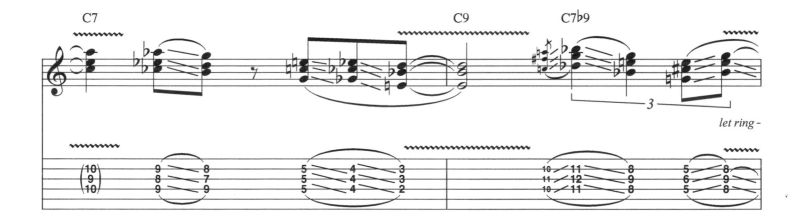

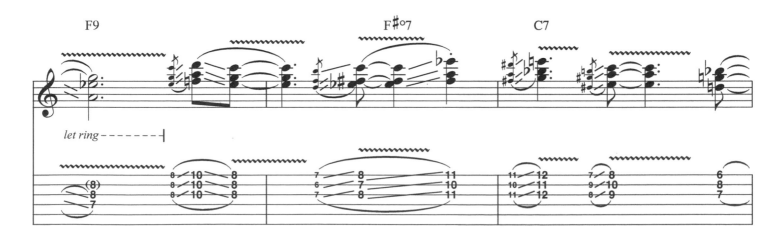

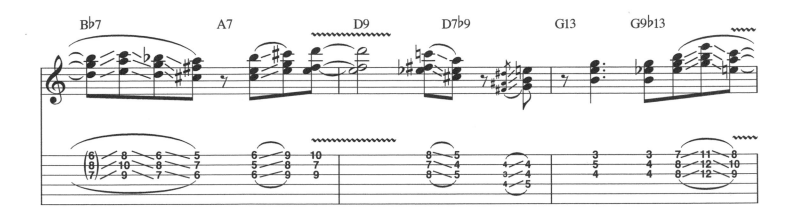

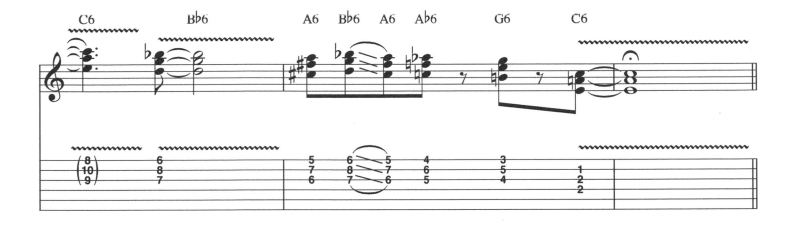

Guitar Instruction
Country Style!
from Hal Leonard

CHICKEN PICKIN' • by Eric Halbig
INCLUDES TAB

This book provides a "bird's-eye-view" of the techniques and licks common to playing hot, country lead guitar! Covers over 100 hot country guitar licks: open-string licks, double-stop licks, scales, string bending, repetitive sequences, and chromatic licks. The online audio includes 99 demonstration tracks with each lick performed at two tempos.

00695599 Book/Online Audio..$17.99

DANIEL DONATO –
THE NEW MASTER OF THE TELECASTER
INCLUDES TAB DVD

PATHWAYS TO DYNAMIC SOLOS

This exclusive instructional book and DVD set includes guitar lessons taught by young Nashville phenom Daniel Donato. The "New Master of the Telecaster" shows you his unique "pathways" concept, opening your mind and fingers to uninhibited fretboard freedom, increased music theory comprehension, and more dynamic solos! The DVD features Daniel Donato himself providing full-band performances and a full hour of guitar lessons, The book includes guitar tab for all the DVD lessons and performances. Topics covered include: using chromatic notes • application of bends • double stops • analyzing different styles • and more. DVD running time: 1 hr., 4 min.

00121923 Book/DVD Pack...$19.99

FRETBOARD ROADMAPS – COUNTRY GUITAR
INCLUDES TAB

The Essential Patterns That All the Pros Know and Use • by Fred Sokolow

This book/CD pack will teach you how to play lead and rhythm in the country style anywhere on the fretboard in any key. You'll play basic country progressions, boogie licks, steel licks, and other melodies and licks. You'll also learn a variety of lead guitar styles using moveable scale patterns, sliding scale patterns, chord-based licks, double-note licks, and more. The book features easy-to-follow diagrams and instructions for beginning, intermediate, and advanced players.

00695353 Book/CD Pack..$16.99

HOW TO PLAY COUNTRY LEAD GUITAR
INCLUDES TAB

by Jeff Adams

Here is a comprehensive stylistic breakdown of country guitar techniques from the past 50 years. Drawing inspiration from the timelessly innovative licks of Merle Travis, Chet Atkins, Albert Lee, Vince Gill, Brent Mason and Brad Paisley, the near 90 musical examples within these pages will hone your left and right hands with technical string-bending and rolling licks while sharpening your knowledge of the thought process behind creating your own licks, and why and when to play them.

00131103 Book/Online Audio...$19.99

COUNTRY LICKS FOR GUITAR
INCLUDES TAB

by Steve Trovato and Jerome Arnold

This unique package examines the lead guitar licks of the masters of country guitar, such as Chet Atkins, Jimmy Bryant, James Burton, Albert Lee, Scotty Moore, and many others! The online audio includes demonstrations of each lick at normal and slow speeds. The instruction covers single-string licks, pedal-steel licks, open-string licks, chord licks, rockabilly licks, funky country licks, tips on fingerings, phrasing, technique, theory, and application.

00695577 Book/Online Audo.............................$19.99

COUNTRY SOLOS
FOR GUITAR
INCLUDES TAB

by Steve Trovato

This unique book/audio pack lets guitarists examine the solo styles of axe masters such as Chet Atkins, James Burton, Ray Flacke, Albert Lee, Scotty Moore, Roy Nichols, Jerry Reed and others. It covers techniques including hot banjo rolls, funky double stops, pedal-steel licks, open-string licks and more, in standard notation and tab with phrase-by-phrase performance notes. The online audio includes full demonstrations and rhythm-only tracks.

00695448 Book/Online Audio.............................$19.99

RED-HOT COUNTRY GUITAR

by Michael Hawley

The complete guide to playing lead guitar in the styles of Pete Anderson, Danny Gatton, Albert Lee, Brent Mason, and more. Includes loads of red-hot licks, techniques, solos, theory and more.

00695831 Book/Online Audio..$19.99

25 GREAT COUNTRY GUITAR SOLOS
INCLUDES TAB

by Dave Rubin

Provides solo transcriptions in notes & tab, lessons on how to play them, guitarist bios, equipment notes, photos, history, and much more. The CD contains full-band demos of every solo in the book. Songs include: Country Boy • Foggy Mountain Special • Folsom Prison Blues • Hellecaster Theme • Hello Mary Lou • I've Got a Tiger by the Tail • The Only Daddy That Will Walk the Line • Please, Please Baby • Sugarfoot Rag • and more.

00699926 Book/CD Pack..$19.99

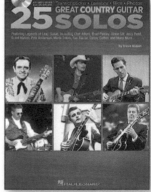

HAL•LEONARD®

www.halleonard.com

Prices, contents, and availability subject to change without notice.